Mike
Craghead
.com

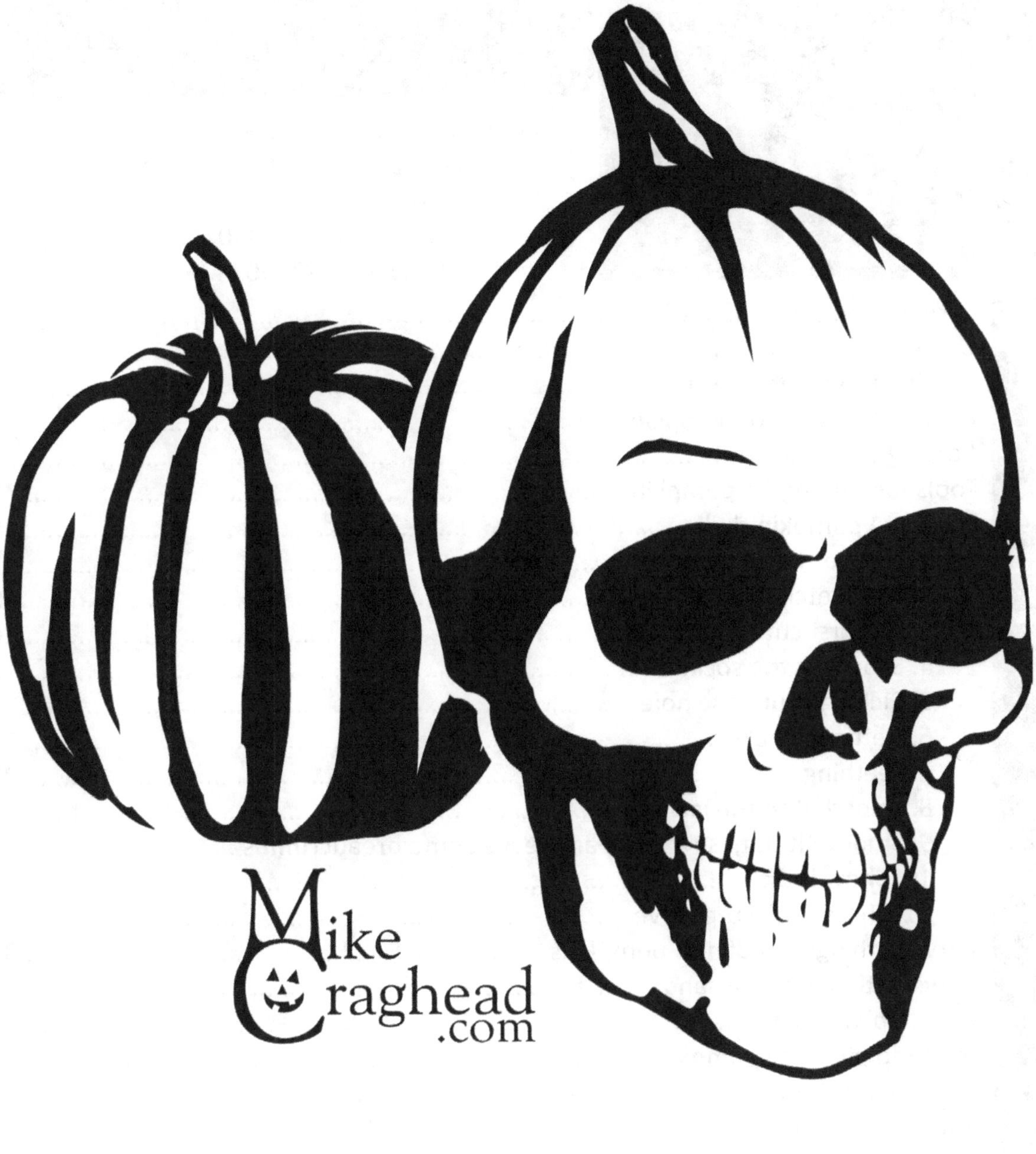

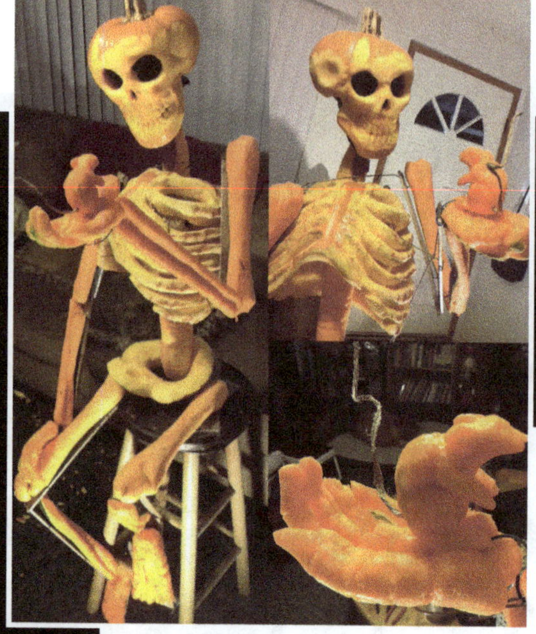

Carving things out of stuff

There's very little difference between carving a pumpkin and carving anything else - you just need to adjust your methods to the medium. Carving is mainly subtractive, meaning you create a cool thing by removing whichever bits aren't cool. Clay is more forgiving because it's both additive and subtractive—you can smoosh a new cool thing onto the cool thing you're making, or you can carve off bits. Pumpkin carving can be a bit of both, but the nice thing is: anything you learn about sculpting anything will help you carve pumpkins. It's all just messing with shapes and forms until they make visual sense. And there are plenty of classes to take, videos to watch, and books to read about sculpture out there. Skip the boring ones, find the ones that look like fun, and gobble them up. That's how everyone learns to carve stuff—even folks who carve marble.

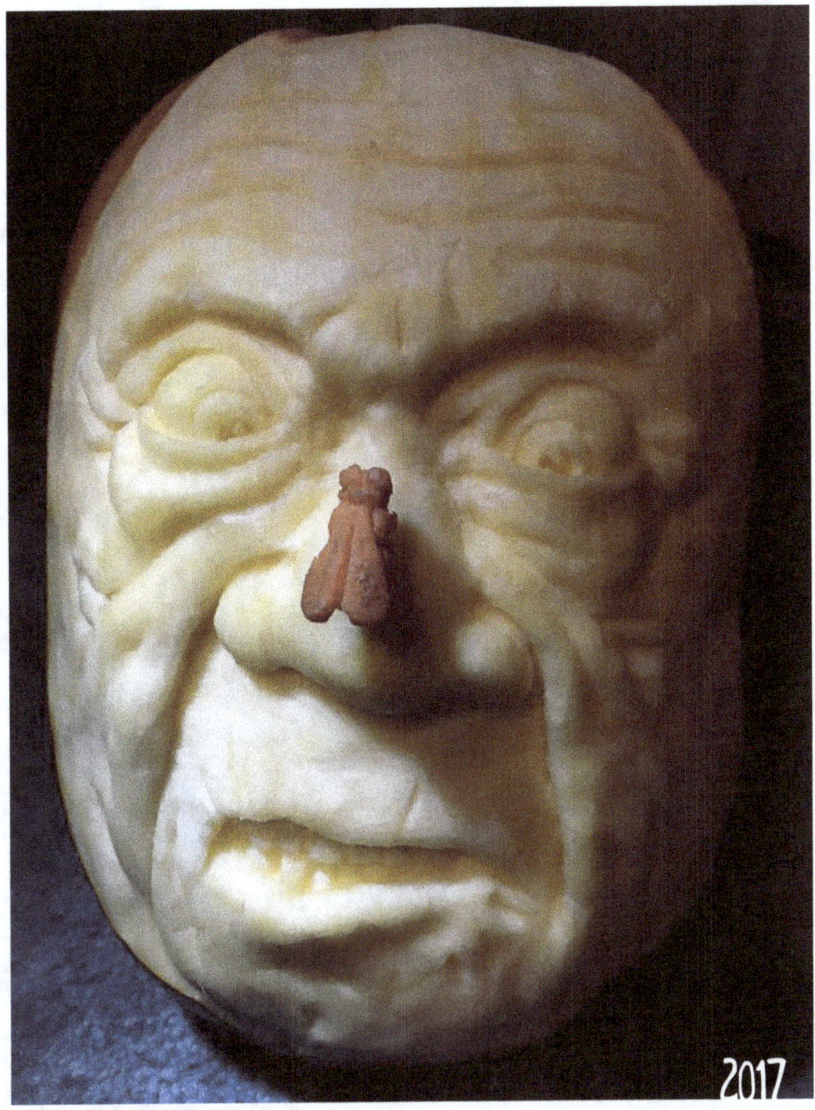

Carving things out of pumpkins

There are plenty of books out there about how to carve pumpkins. You should read them. And carve lots of pumpkins, because everyone likes carved pumpkins. In fact, I think lots of people like carved pumpkins better than they like carvings made of less squishy materials like wood or stone. Nowadays most folks are only mildly impressed when confronted with a marble masterpiece, maybe because they've never tried playing with marble and they just figure it's something other folks do, and they don't feel invited to the party. Or does it have to do with the fact that we've largely removed our art from curriculums and locked it away in galleries? But a pumpkin is familiar and approach-able, and most folks have played with one. And they know that to spend a lot of time and energy carving a pumpkin is inherently absurd, because they know it's doomed to become mush. But they get it. And they like it. Despite, and because of, the absurdity.

It's the same with sand sculpture. And fancy cakes, and candy, and cheese, and butter. The foolishness of making something remarkable out of familiar material with a short lifespan somehow manages to invite everyone to the party. Maybe the fact that fewer folks will see it makes people like it more? It becomes an experience shared by a select few, brought together only by their mutual presence in a given moment. That's why live music and theater are so compelling, right? And imagine how much more compelling live performance would be if we knew everyone on stage was about to turn to mush four days after the show!

Wait, don't imagine that. It's dumb.

But no matter how this particular brand of silly art reaches folks, via TV or web video or a live carving demo at a pumpkin patch or a compelling gourd on a porch, it does reach them. It reaches them whether they have an art degree, or they're convinced they can't draw. No one's going to put a pumpkin in a gallery because that's super gross and moldy, but everyone likes pumpkins.

Carving faces out of stuff

It's always helpful to use references, particularly when you're making a face. So if you're doing that, one option is to use the drawings on pages 13-15 to get some proportional "rules" for faces and skulls. Other options include doing an image search on the googlywebnets, or forcing your friends sit in front of you for hours while they make a weird face (recommended for friends you're not very fond of).

But regardless of the reference, for each facial feature, it's your decision to either break the rules or to follow them. That applies to every face you make, whether it's human or semi-human, with or without skin. Sometimes it's best to try to follow all the rules, especially when you're trying for a likeness of a specific person, or like we're doing in this book, a human skull. But what about a mutant or a goblin or an alien or a mutant goblin alien? Look at images of your favorite scary monsters, and figure out what individual features give you the creeps: are the eyes too far apart, too big or too small? Is one missing, or are they two different sizes? Or are there too damn many? Those rules and many others have been either followed or broken by the designer of every scary monster, and you get to do the same thing when you're carving pumpkins or anything else. So keep the rules in mind, and either follow them or break them, for specific reasons.

a study in clay from 1989 or so. clay folks can start with a skull and add muscles and other stuff until they end up with a face, but pumpkin folks can't.

Carving faces out of pumpkins

I won't be providing you with any step-by-step instructions for a pumpkin face. Because while I'm sure you'd end up with a face that looked a lot like the face I made, and you might learn something new, I'd have to choose a specific face to show you how to make. And that doesn't sound like much fun, because although themes recur (like "grouchy, squinty dude"), I never really haul off and repeat a pumpkin design because I have the attention span of a gnat.

The only design I repeat a lot is a skull, which is why I feel like I can show you how to do that.

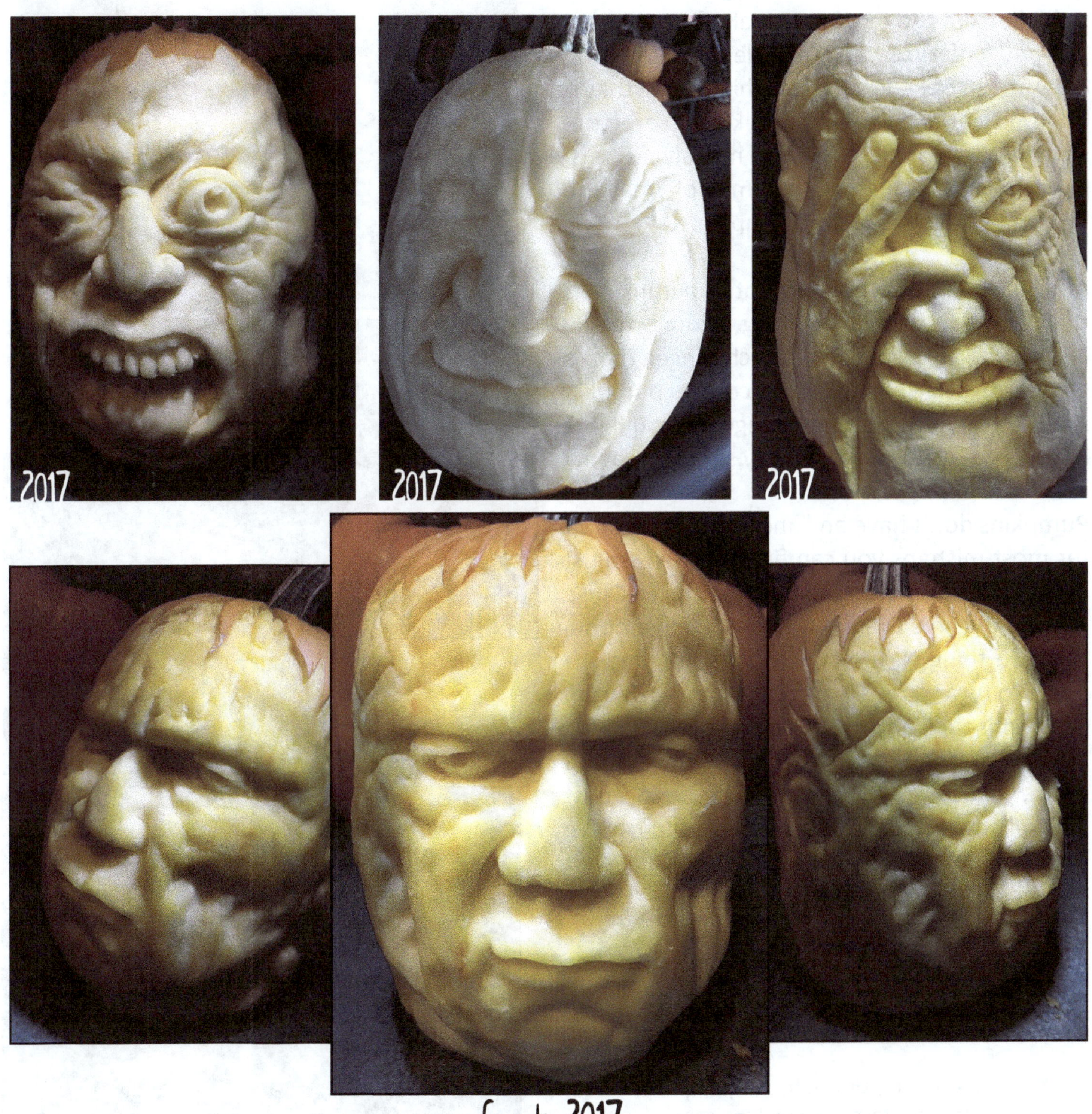

Carving 3D pumpkins

Personally, I'm not interested in carving the kind of super-detailed shaded pumpkins that light up from the inside. There are lots of folks doing amazing work in that field, and I tip my hat to them! But I find it frustrating and unforgiving and every time I've tried it, it's made me feel stabby*. So, I prefer carving things meant to be lit from the outside; usually faces of people and creatures and people-creatures and creature-people. It's a weird thing to do that is done primarily by weirdos: folks who are constant sources of inspiration to me, always raising the bar and pushing the limits of what can be done with an ordinary pumpkin.

Another benefit to relief-sculpted pumpkins is that if you can avoid breaking through to the inside, your work will live much longer than a standard jack-o'-lantern. Of course pumpkin skulls don't have that advantage, so you'll just have to get used to a relatively short lifespan.

Pumpkins don't have an "undo" button, but after most mishaps you can find a way to adjust on-the-fly and make something work. Because while you can't truly undo what you've done, the nice thing is: it's only a pumpkin, and it's going to turn to mush. So you get to learn from every mishap. And if you want a particularly grievous mishap to vanish from the face of the earth, just don't take pictures! Your compost bin will never reveal its secrets, and you've learned something you can use on your next pumpkin.

That said, get a compost bin. Or make friends with your neighbor who has one. Because mush management can be challenging.

*If you want to try those shaded pumpkins, a good place to start is **stoneykins.com**.

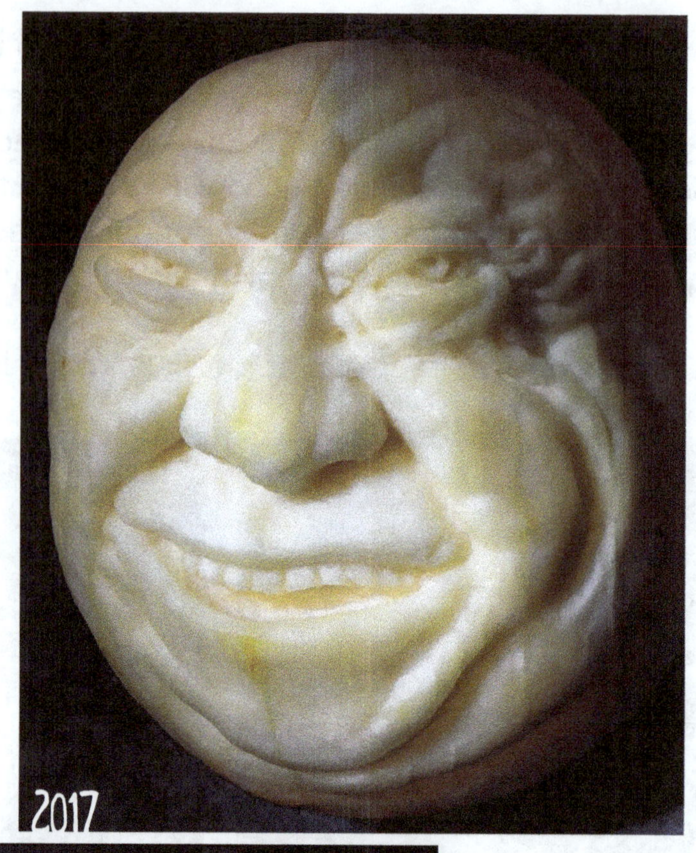

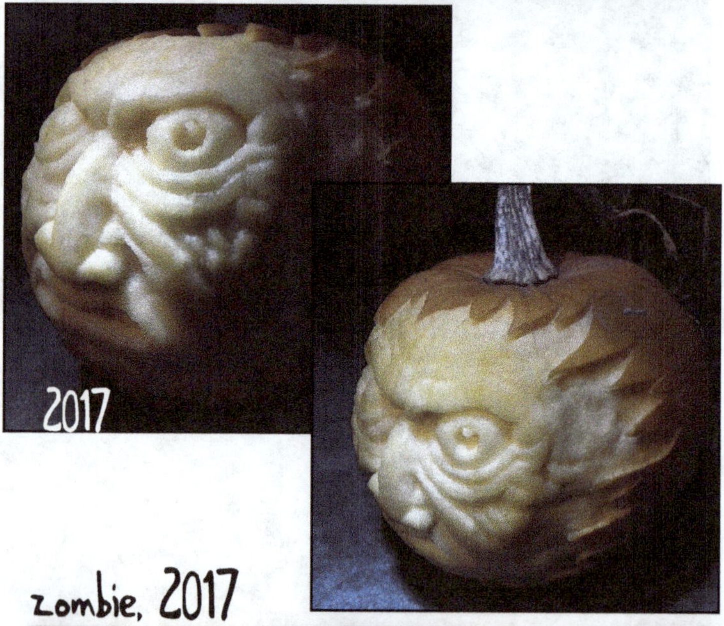

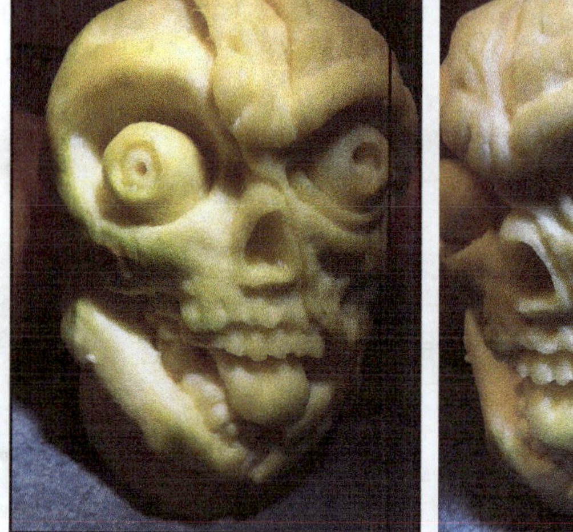

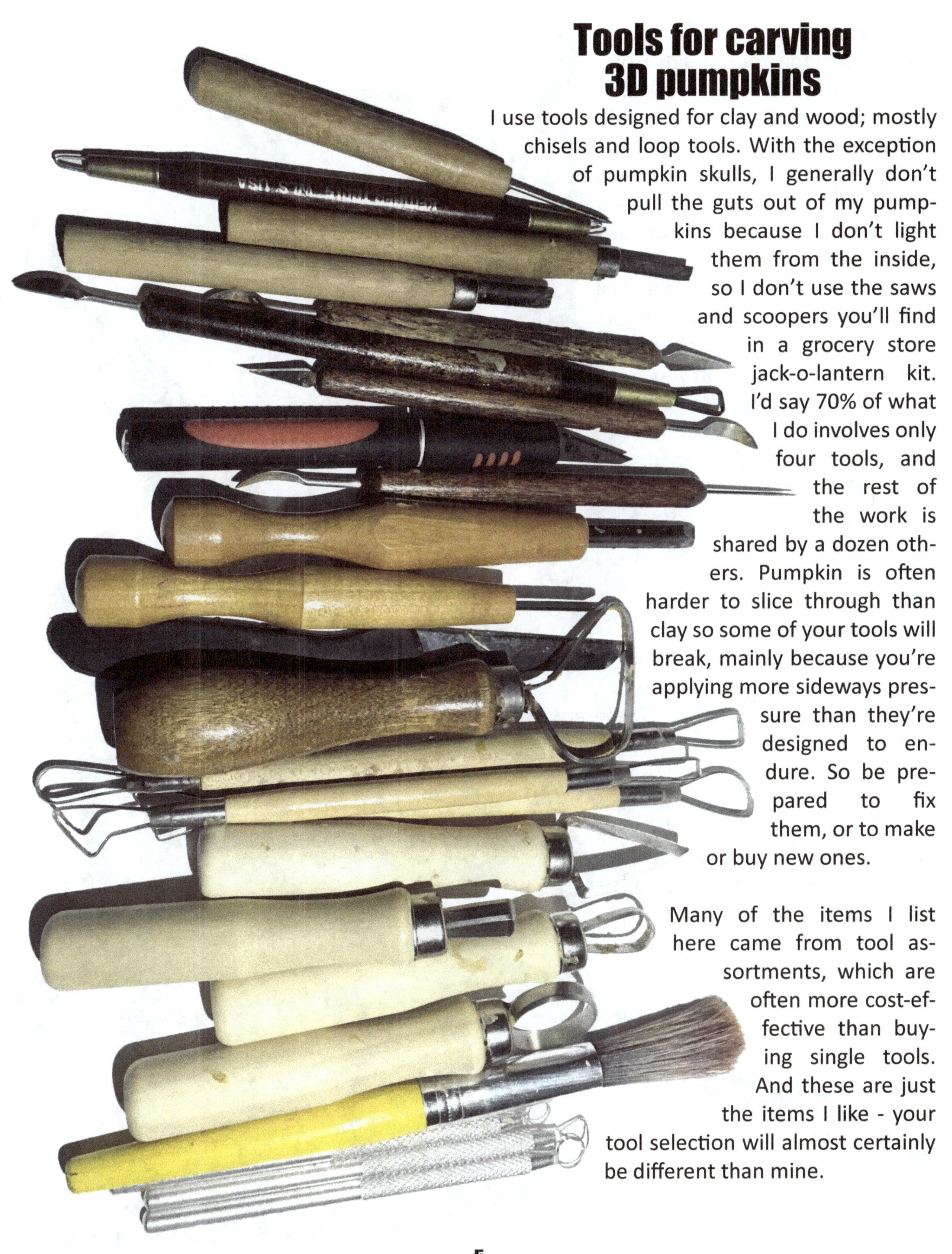

Tools for carving 3D pumpkins

I use tools designed for clay and wood; mostly chisels and loop tools. With the exception of pumpkin skulls, I generally don't pull the guts out of my pumpkins because I don't light them from the inside, so I don't use the saws and scoopers you'll find in a grocery store jack-o-lantern kit. I'd say 70% of what I do involves only four tools, and the rest of the work is shared by a dozen others. Pumpkin is often harder to slice through than clay so some of your tools will break, mainly because you're applying more sideways pressure than they're designed to endure. So be prepared to fix them, or to make or buy new ones.

Many of the items I list here came from tool assortments, which are often more cost-effective than buying single tools. And these are just the items I like - your tool selection will almost certainly be different than mine.

My must-haves:

-Large clay loop tool: a sideways-egg-shaped flat wire with a wooden handle. There are lots of other shapes, but the sideways-egg is the most common. These are indispensable for the first pass, either peeling the outer skin or gobbling up large chunks at once and leaving behind smooth cuts. But they're the first tool you'll break. And it's not their fault, it's yours. You're asking too much of them. Shame on you.

-Small clay loop tool: often double-sided, either an oval- or rounded rectangle-shaped blade. These are quite versatile and a bit less prone to breakage than their larger siblings.

-Right-angle or square wood chisel: with a v-shaped cutting head, often used for the first cuts, tracing lines drawn on a pumpkin.

-Small, sharp, curved blade: These are a little harder to find, and are often grouped in assortments with other "cleanup tools." Some are double-sided with a straight blade or needle at the other end, but the part I tend to use most for details and finishing is that curved blade. Both edges are sharp, so be careful!

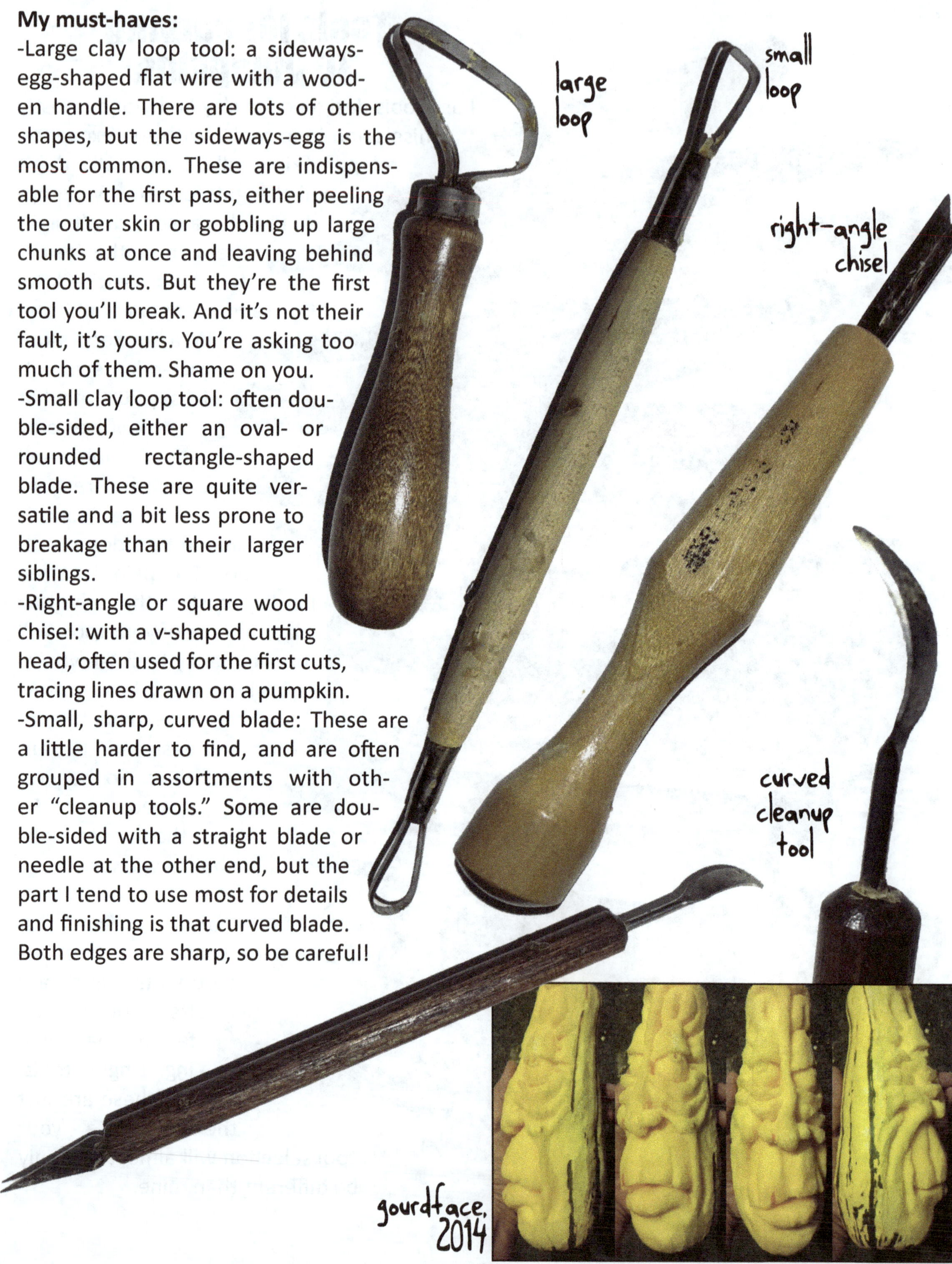

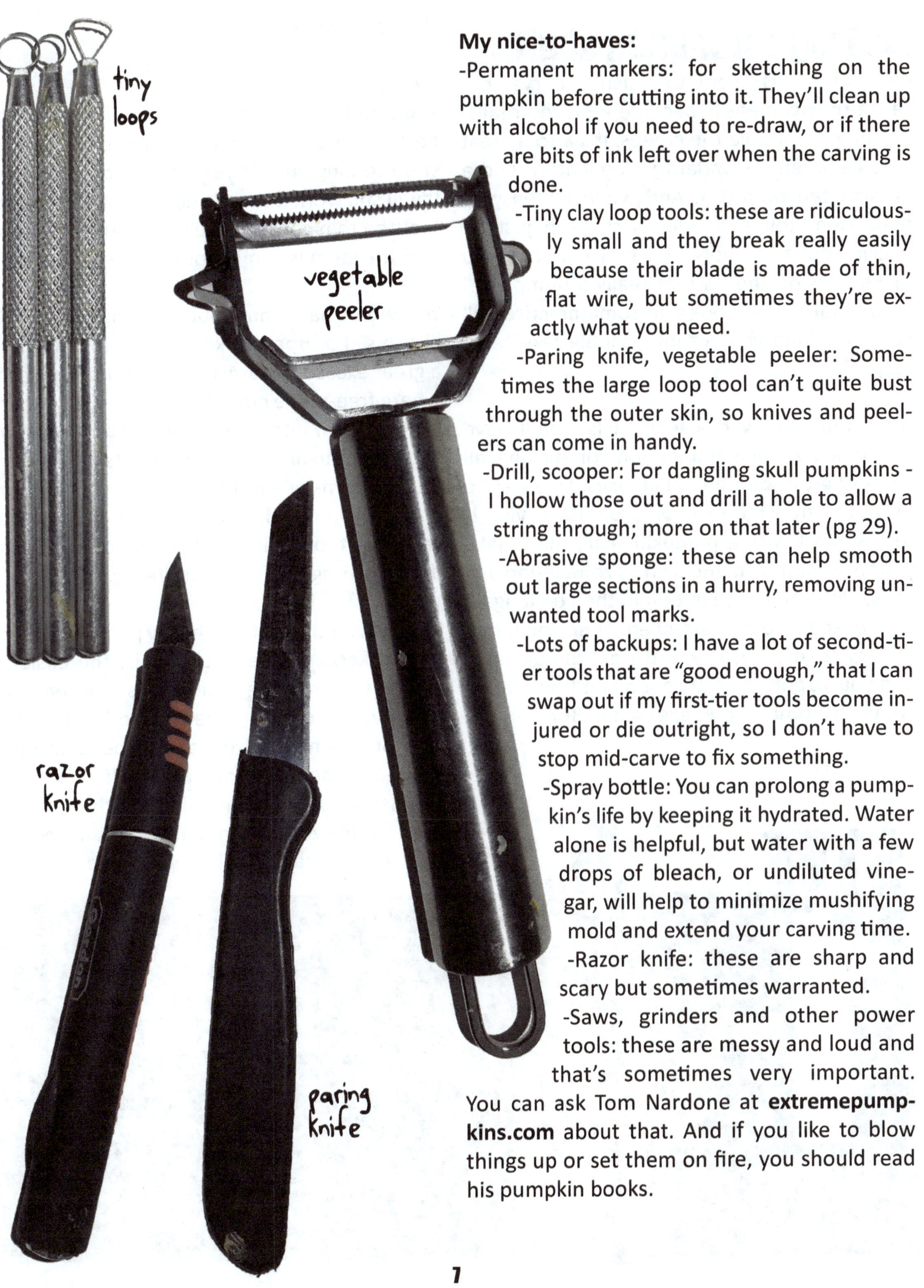

My nice-to-haves:
-Permanent markers: for sketching on the pumpkin before cutting into it. They'll clean up with alcohol if you need to re-draw, or if there are bits of ink left over when the carving is done.

-Tiny clay loop tools: these are ridiculously small and they break really easily because their blade is made of thin, flat wire, but sometimes they're exactly what you need.

-Paring knife, vegetable peeler: Sometimes the large loop tool can't quite bust through the outer skin, so knives and peelers can come in handy.

-Drill, scooper: For dangling skull pumpkins - I hollow those out and drill a hole to allow a string through; more on that later (pg 29).

-Abrasive sponge: these can help smooth out large sections in a hurry, removing unwanted tool marks.

-Lots of backups: I have a lot of second-tier tools that are "good enough," that I can swap out if my first-tier tools become injured or die outright, so I don't have to stop mid-carve to fix something.

-Spray bottle: You can prolong a pumpkin's life by keeping it hydrated. Water alone is helpful, but water with a few drops of bleach, or undiluted vinegar, will help to minimize mushifying mold and extend your carving time.

-Razor knife: these are sharp and scary but sometimes warranted.

-Saws, grinders and other power tools: these are messy and loud and that's sometimes very important. You can ask Tom Nardone at **extremepumpkins.com** about that. And if you like to blow things up or set them on fire, you should read his pumpkin books.

Making a pumpkin skull:

Pumpkin skulls seem to touch a nerve, because they can easily become a bit too realistic and give people the creeps. It's also a great step between a standard jack-o'lantern and a 3D-sculpted pumpkin. And while it's easy to make something that looks skull-ish just by hacking out a few holes, it's more fun to try to make folks do the "is that really a pumpkin?" double-take. This book and some practice will definitely help you get into double-take territory!

After you've carved a few skulls, you'll have developed a solid foundation for making all kinds of grotesque pumpkin faces. One way to make the transition to non-skull 3D carving is to first start with a pumpkin skull, then make your next pumpkin into a gross zombie-looking thing with some face left on it, then do it again with even more face attached. Then you'll find that you're making an entire gross zombie face, and you've gotten pretty good at it (there are a couple of zombies on pages 4 and 36).

Here's how to do it:

Step 1. Pick your pumpkin
You need a head-sized, pear-shaped one. It's best if you can find one with a great big loopy stem coming out of the thick end of the "pear." It will still work if there's no stem or if the stem is at the thin end, but the end result is far cooler if the stem is coming out of the top.

You won't have much luck finding a pumpkin like this at a supermarket, I'm afraid. But that's a great excuse to go visit a rural pumpkin patch where free-range pumpkins roam and are more likely to grow into weird shapes. I'm pretty sure all the pumpkins in supermarkets come from factory farms where the pumpkins barely have enough room to flap their wings because the cages are too small. I could have some of those details wrong, but I don't think so.

The heavier the better: a heavy pumpkin means it's thicker, and the thicker it is, the easier it will be to mimic the dimensions of a real skull when you're carving. There are a lot of immature pumpkins that manage to become pear-shaped without getting very thick at all - you can use those in a pinch (in fact, that's what I used for my 2007 Instructable), but it's best to stick with a heavy one if you can find it.

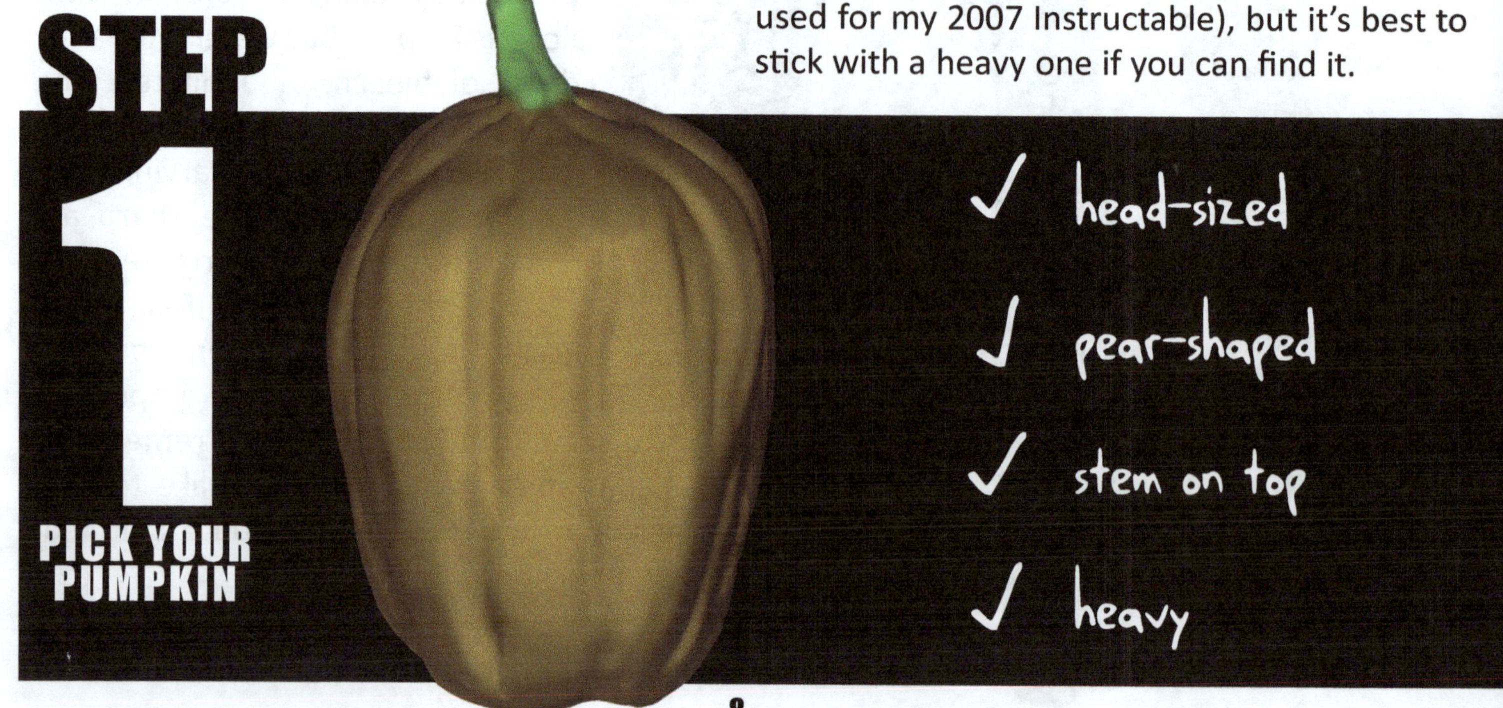

If you can't find a sufficiently pear-shaped pumpkin that wants to be a skull, look for a head-sized butternut squash. It won't be quite as cool and halloweeny as a pumpkin, but it's nice and thick and is a passable pear-shaped pumpkin impersonator.

I posted a pumpkin skull tutorial on Instructables.com back in 2007. If you're curious it's still up there (follow the link below if you're so inclined), but it was done with nothing but a paring knife so it's a bit too faceted to be convincing. It still reads as a skull, but if you can scare up some clay tools and a little more patience than I had back then, your results will be much better than mine were.

instructables.com/id/Skull-Pumpkin 

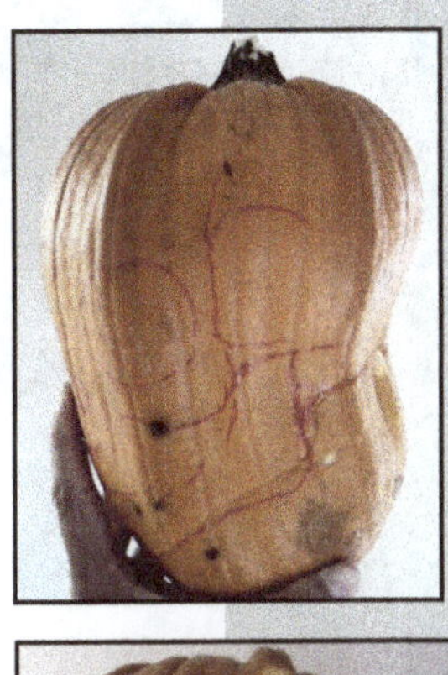
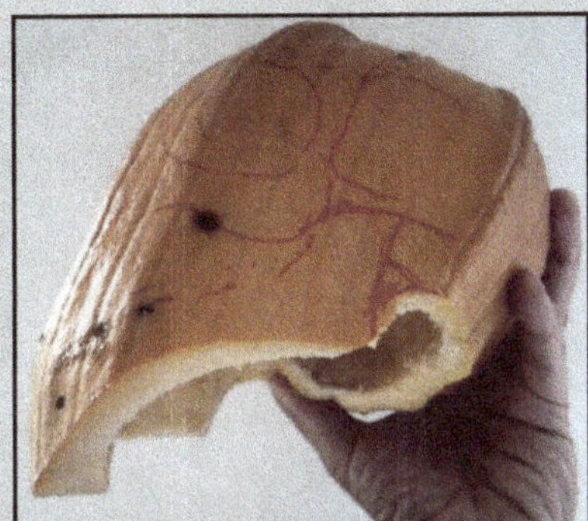
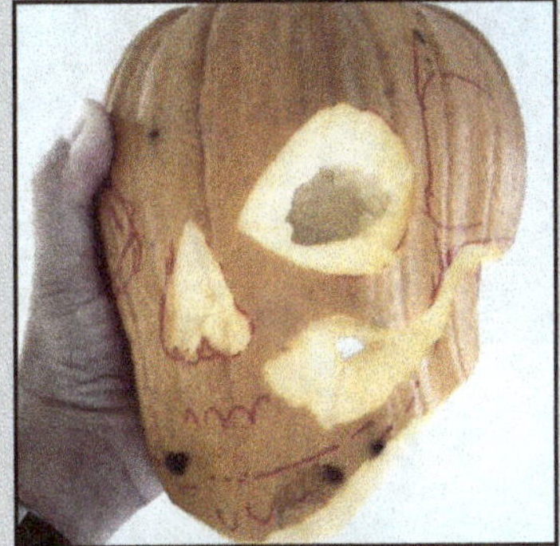
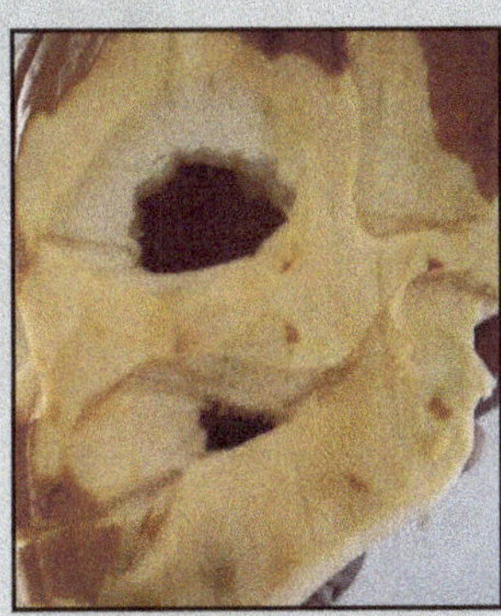
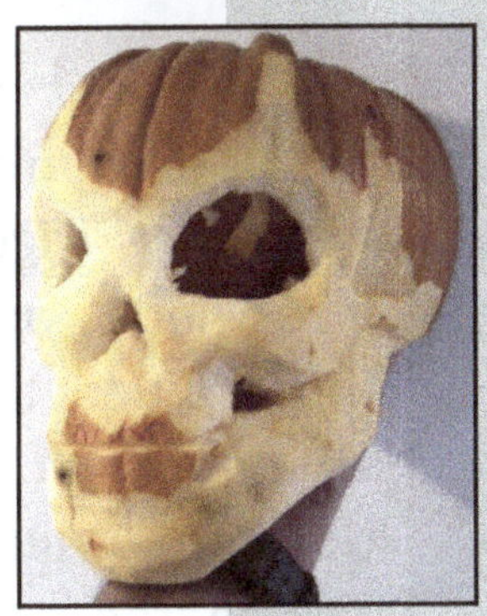
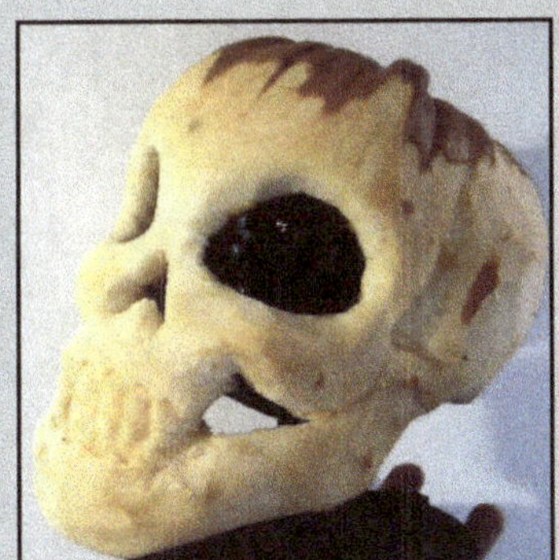
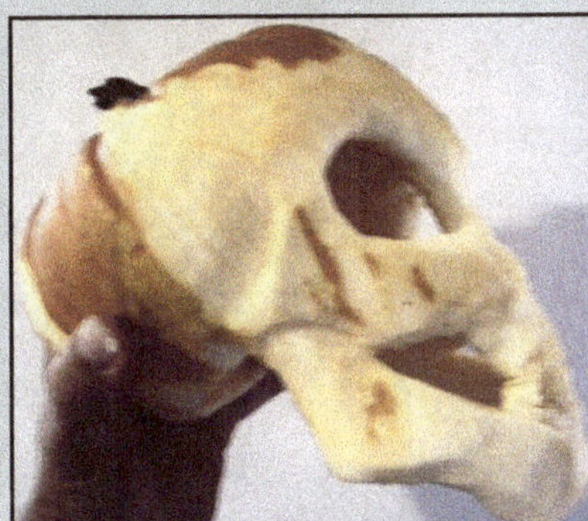
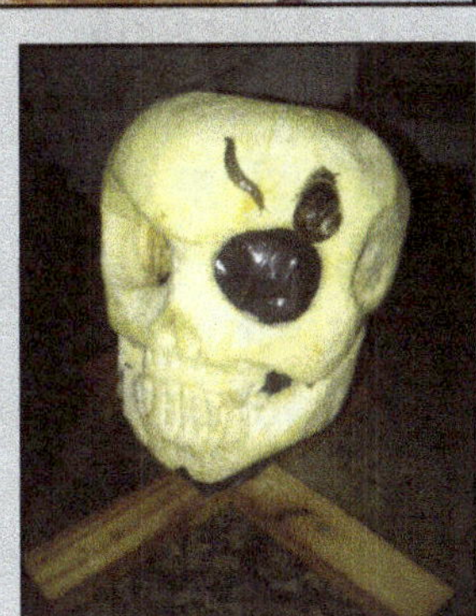

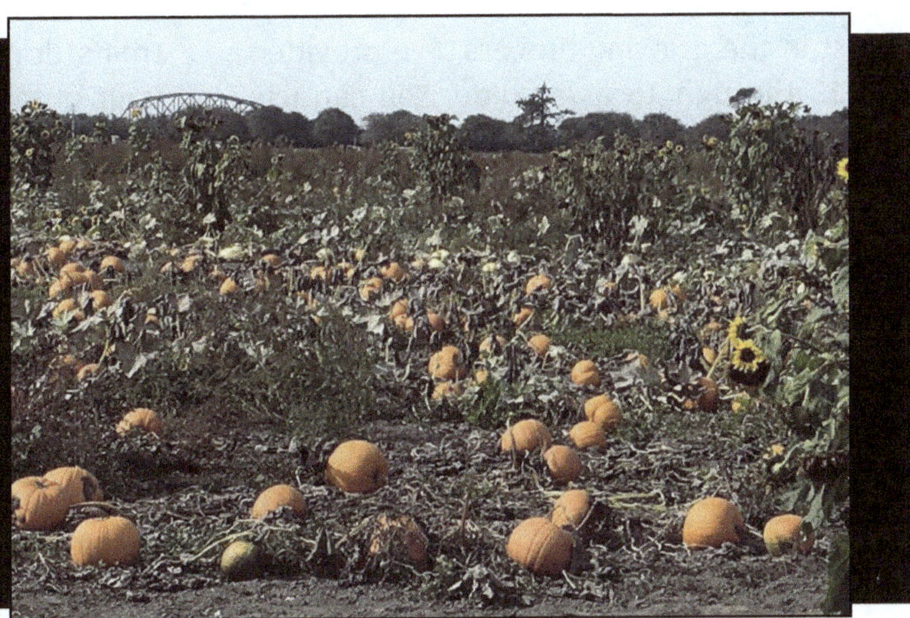

STEP

2

GET SKETCHY

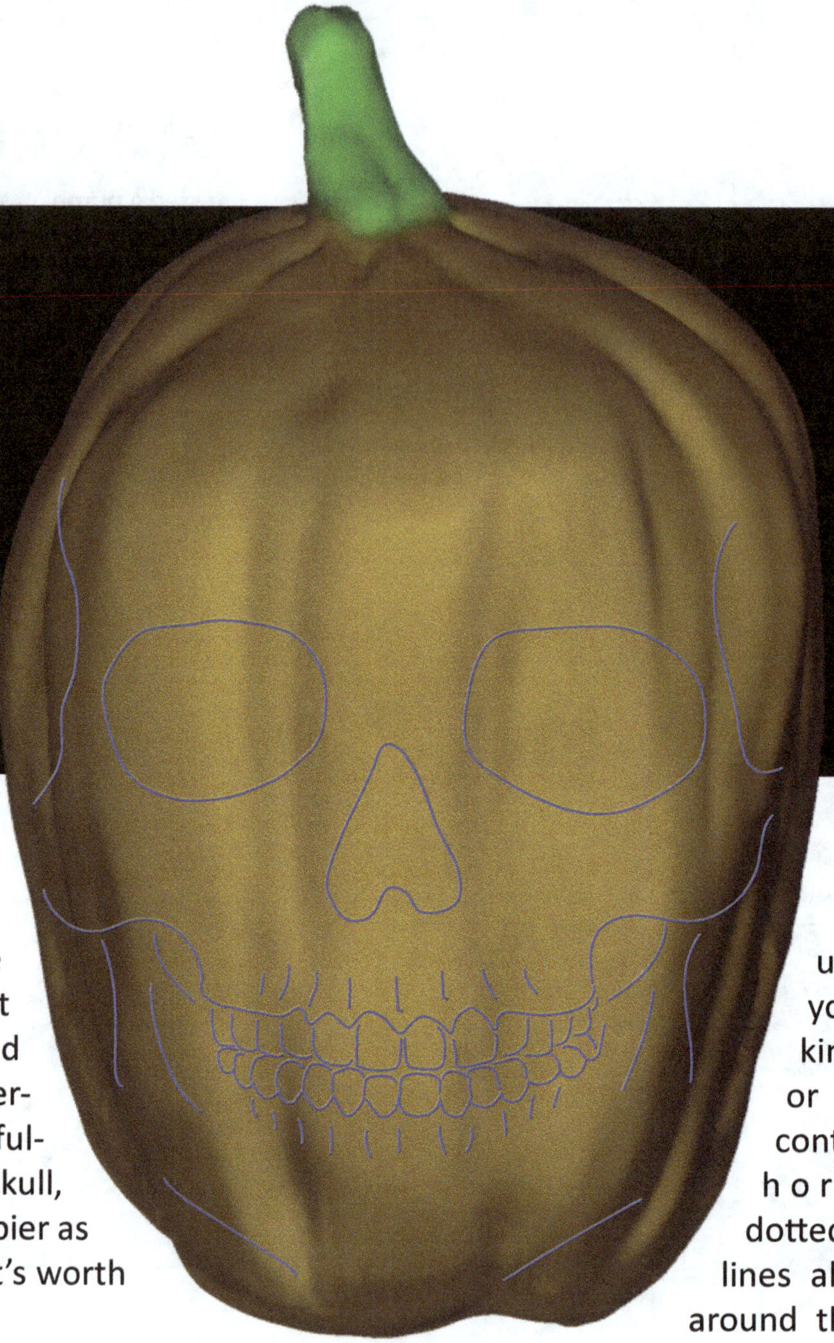

Step 2. Get sketchy

Draw the skull onto the pumpkin using a permanent marker. Again, you don't need to execute the anatomy perfectly for your pumpkin to be fully recognizable as a human skull, but I think it or becomes creepier as you get more realistic, so that's worth striving for.

To assist in the drawing process, I've provided pages 13 through 15 as a guide. You can use them in at least two different ways:

1. Hold the book up to your pumpkin and transfer the straight lines, then sketch the features of the skull inside those lines.

It will be easier if you can find two different-colored fine-tipped permanent markers - one for the lines, one for the sketching. Rest your pumpkin in your lap or on a table (if it tries to roll away, place it in a towel curled into a donut shape). Then hold this book up next to your pumpkin (right or left), and continue the horizontal dotted guidelines all the way around the surface of your pumpkin. When that's done, move the book to the top of your pumpkin and extend the vertical lines down the face. Then turn the page and your pumpkin, and draw the vertical lines down the sides.

When the straight guidelines are done, draw your skull using your second color marker. You can then erase the straight lines using alcohol if you like.

2. Don't draw on the pumpkin at all, just refer to the illustrations as you carve.

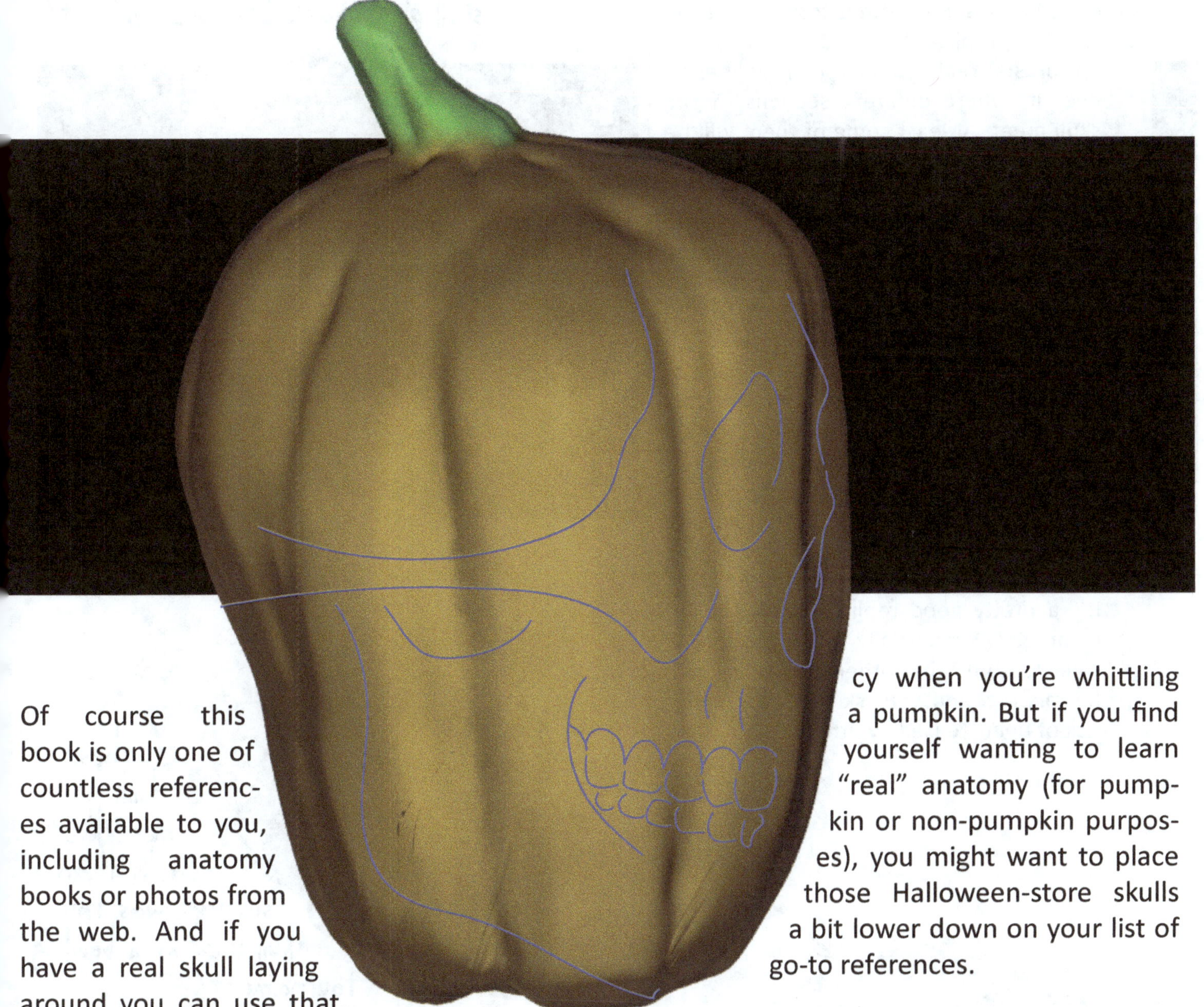

Of course this book is only one of countless references available to you, including anatomy books or photos from the web. And if you have a real skull laying around you can use that, but I must ask: what are you doing with a real human skull, you weirdo?

Note: If you happen to have a non-real skull laying around, like a novelty skull made of plastic or styrofoam that you found at a Halloween or craft store, here's one very minor item to consider: These almost always have a few anatomical "mistakes." Nothing dramatically wrong; just a few wonky proportions, or some liberties were taken to simplify the mold-making process, or some tweaks were made to make the skull look "mean." They all read loud-and-clear as "human skull" so it may not matter, and you'll of course never achieve perfect accura-

cy when you're whittling a pumpkin. But if you find yourself wanting to learn "real" anatomy (for pumpkin or non-pumpkin purposes), you might want to place those Halloween-store skulls a bit lower down on your list of go-to references.

Also keep in mind that there is a lot of variation in real skulls, and even more if you decide you're making a monster or alien or something. So the references and tips in this book (or any other source) are only a starting point. Feel free to follow your references as closely or as loosely you like, it's all up to you, but your end result is better if you always have a specific reason for breaking a rule. Sometimes the reason is, "the pumpkin made me do it" because pumpkins can be bossy jerks. But the rest of the time, feel free to stray a bit from standard proportions, especially if you've decided that something other than a standard human used to wear your skull under its non-standard face.

Here are two a simple litmus tests for the accuracy of any replica skull:

-Sutures: A real skull has squiggly lines all over it, where different sections of the skull meet. At least some of them will be missing from any less-than-accurate skull.

-Foramina: A real skull has little holes in it where nerves pass through the skull and then branch out across the face where they can do various nervy activities. They usually come in pairs and are easy to find if you're looking for them, but are often missing from a "fake" skull. Three pairs of these holes are right up in front: one tiny pair is at the top of each eyebrow (called supraorbital foramen), one is on either side of the nasal cavity (infraorbital foramen), and the largest pair is on either side of the chin (mental foramen). If your skull has all three sets, chances are better that it's a pretty good replica. But if they're completely or partially missing, you can safely assume that other details will also be missing, and your skull is at a higher risk of being teased by other skulls.

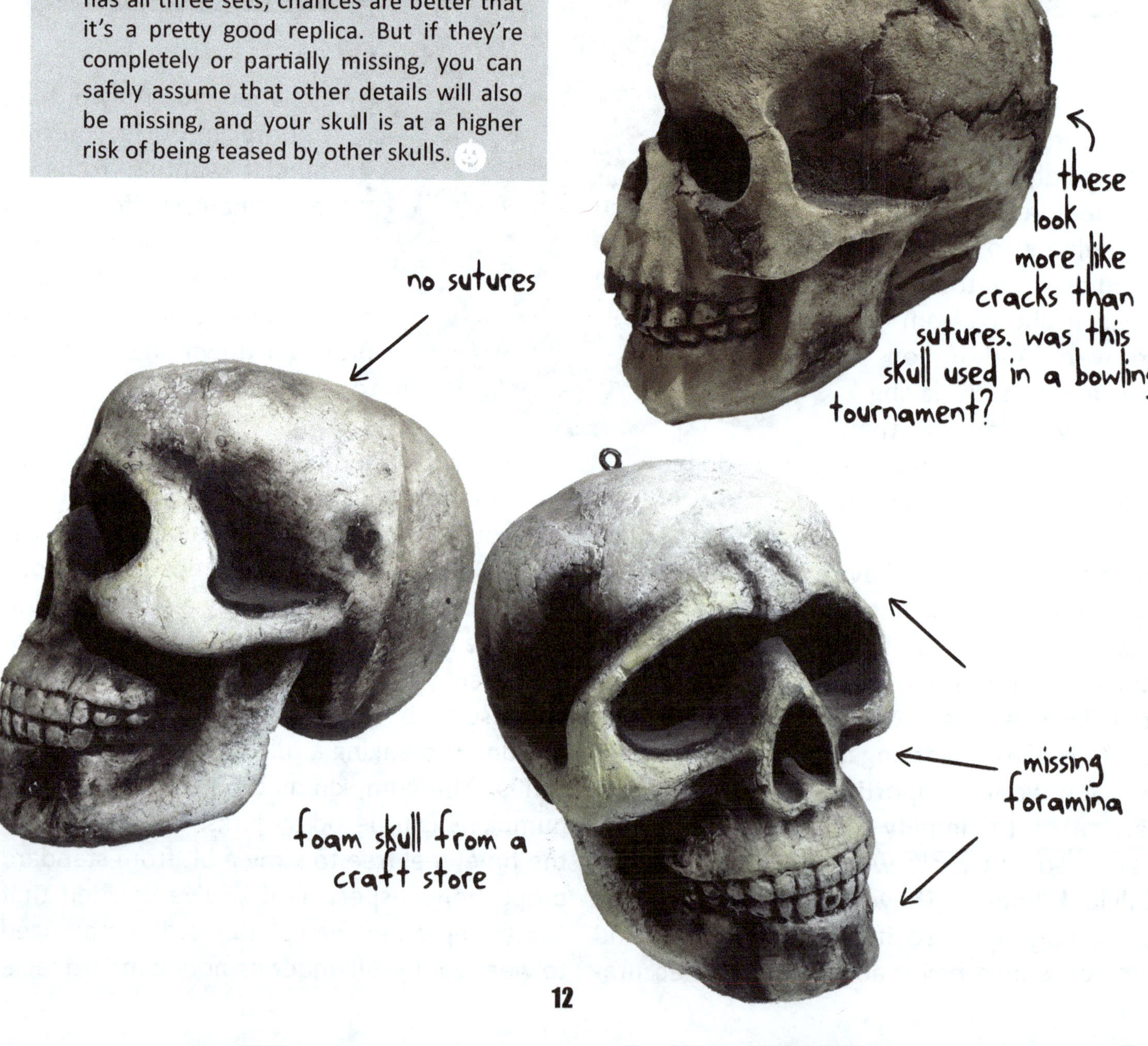

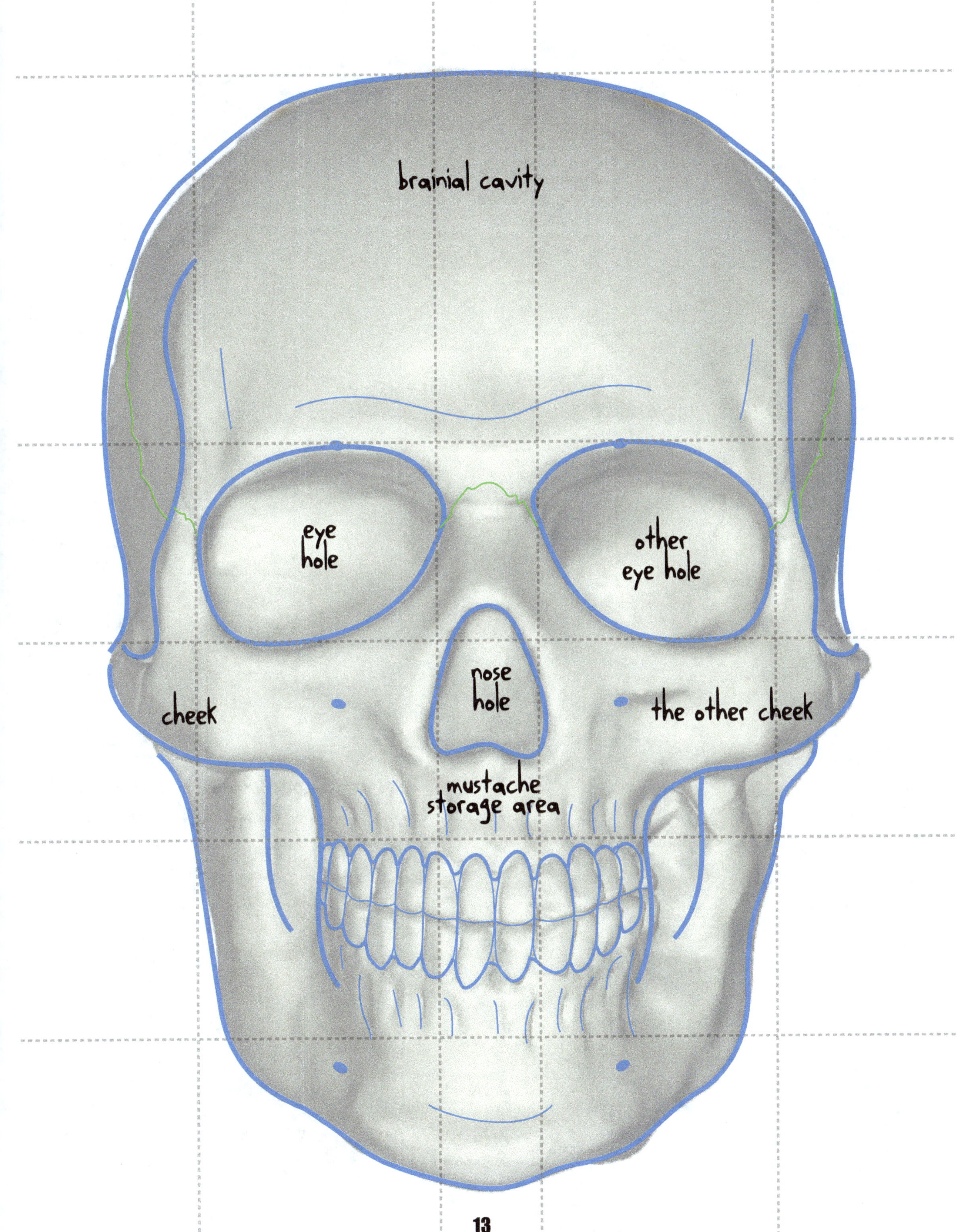
brainial cavity
eye hole
other eye hole
nose hole
cheek
the other cheek
mustache storage area

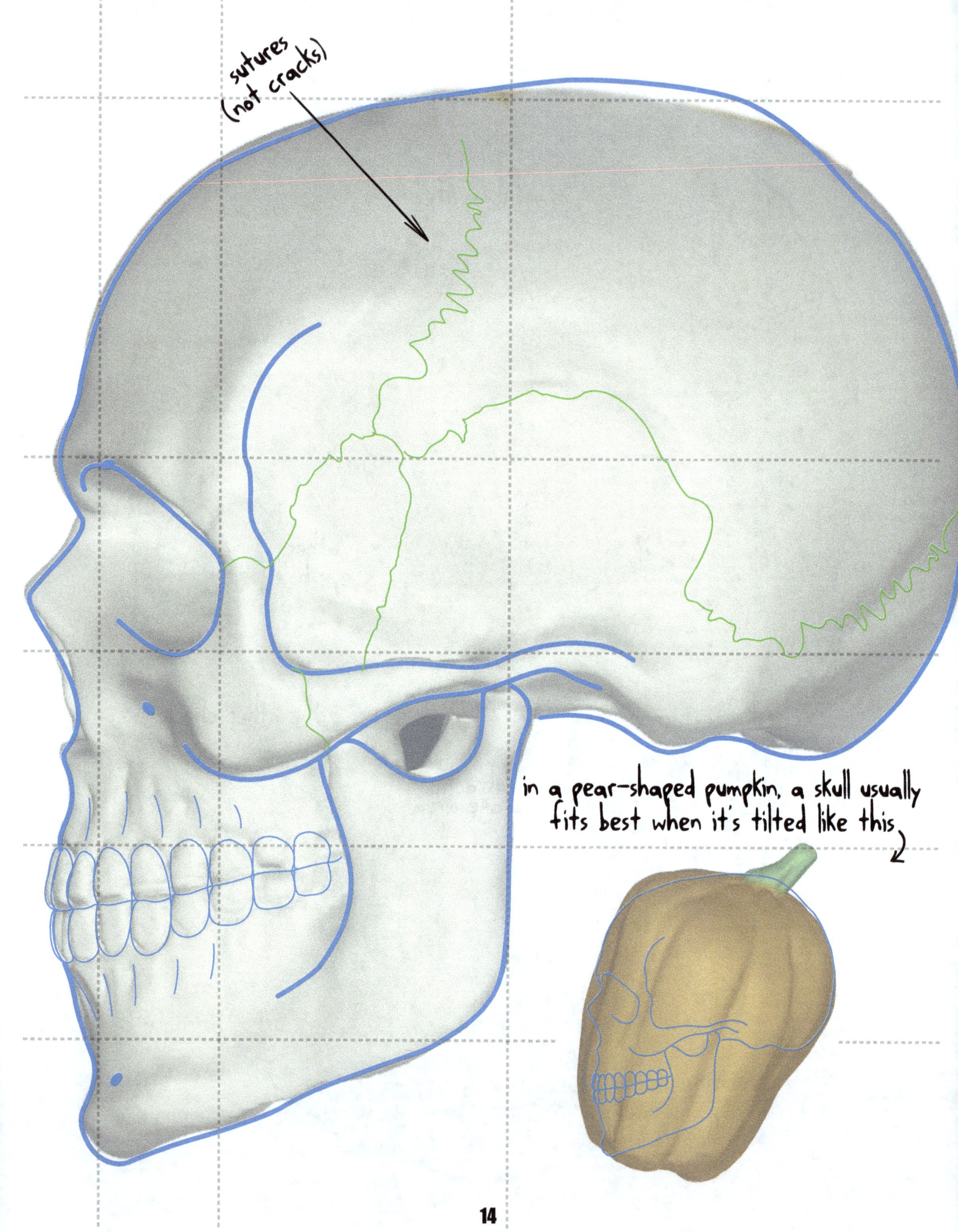

sutures
(not cracks)
in a pear-shaped pumpkin, a skull usually
fits best when it's tilted like this

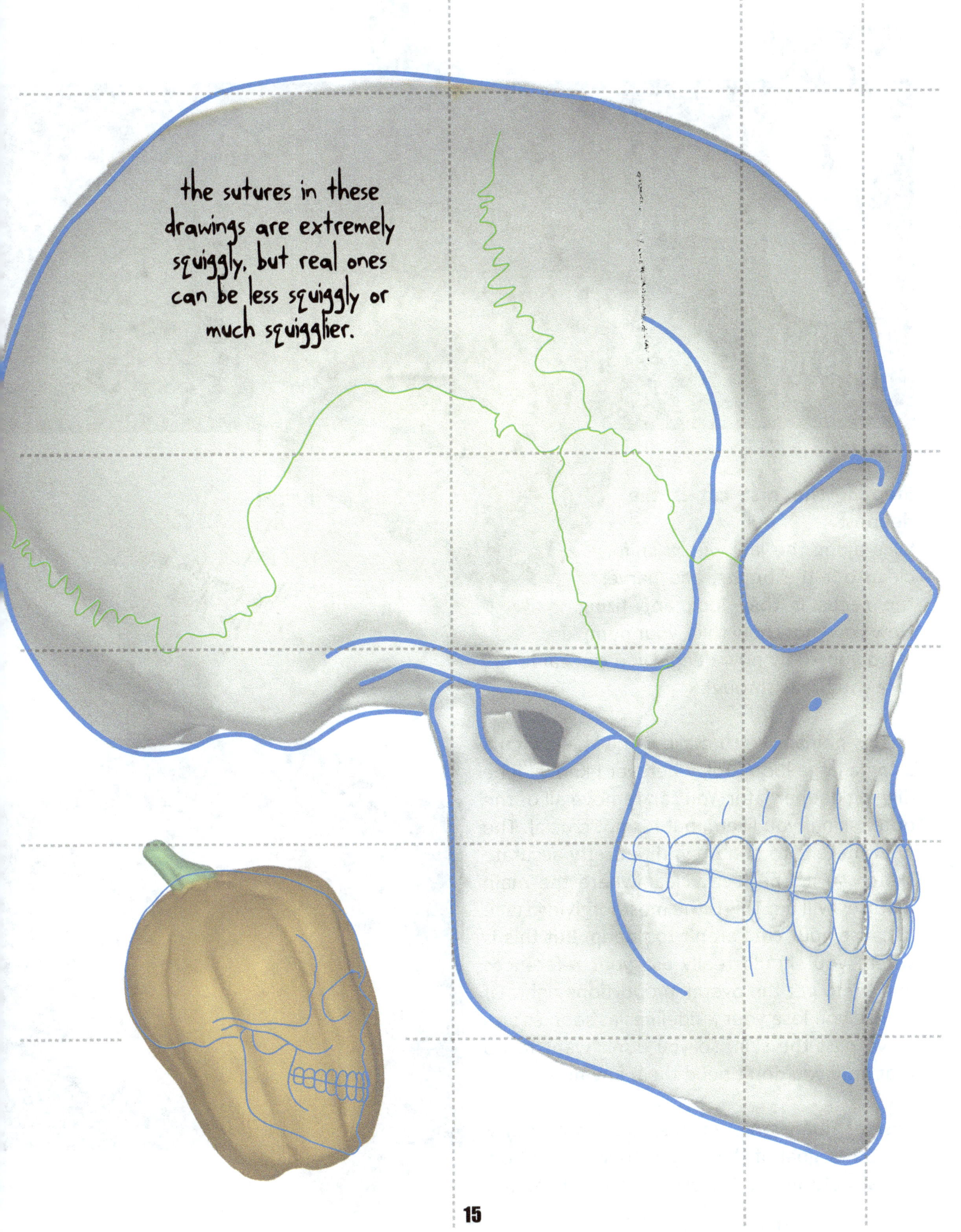

the sutures in these
drawings are extremely
squiggly, but real ones
can be less squiggly or
much squigglier.

STEP 3

THE FIRST CUT IS THE DEEPEST

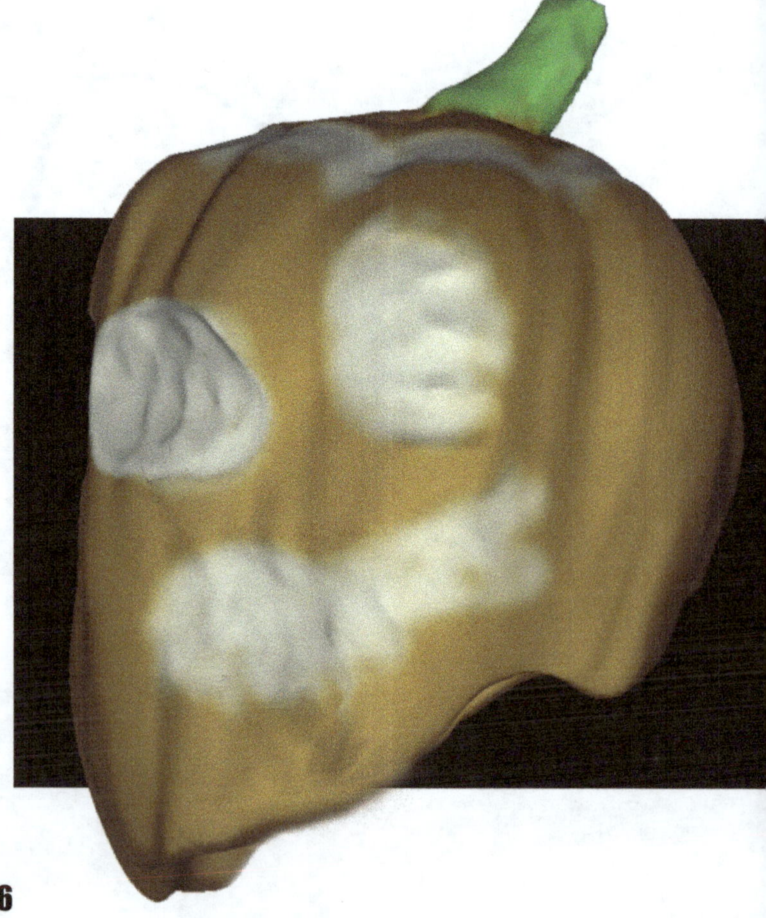

Step 3. The first cut is the deepest

Slice along the jaw with a knife, clean out the brains, and harvest the seeds if they look appetizing. Now you know how thick your pumpkin is, so you know how deeply you can carve before you break through.

At this point I like to make some shallow cuts using a large loop tool, wherever I know I'll be digging deeper later. You can remove all of the outer skin if you likem, but it's not crucial. The point here is to end up with a pretty accurate sketch so it's perfectly clear where the main features will be. This is the most forgiving stage because your cuts aren't too deep, but this is where you should really use your references and try to get the overall proportions right. Of course you lose your guidelines as soon as you carve past the skin, so you don't want to do that until you don't need them anymore.

Besides managing your skull's proportions, the other goal of this step is to spell out how the structures are "stacked," as in what's far-

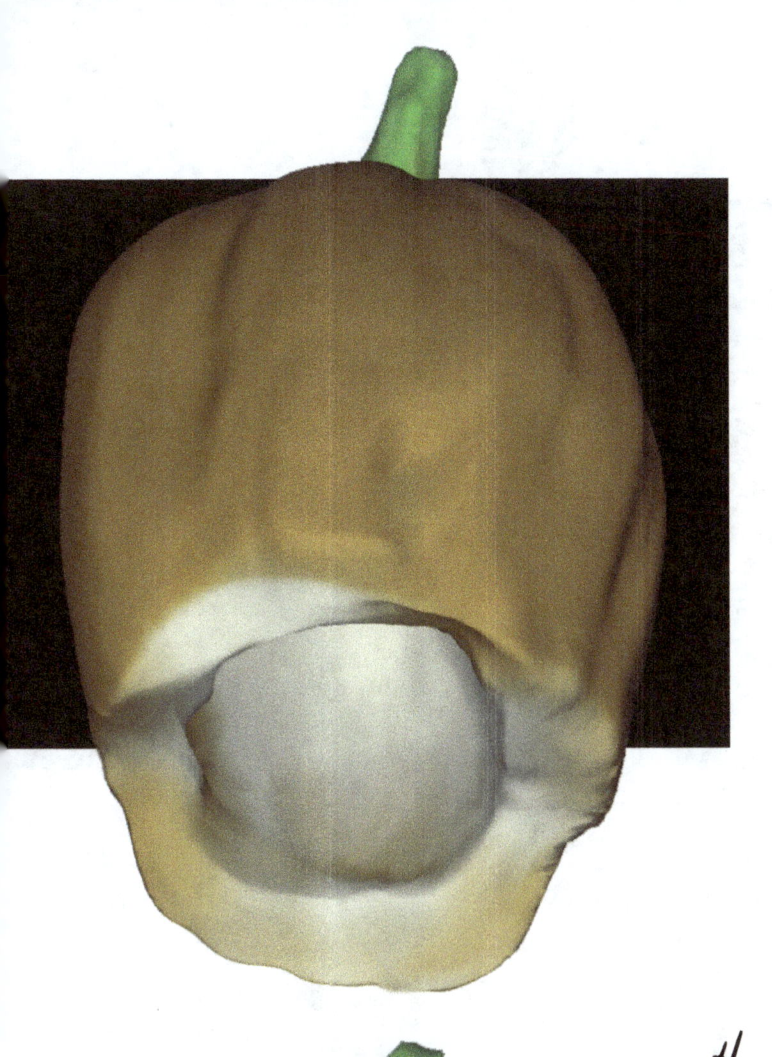

thest out, where the deepest cuts will go, and what's on top of what. For instance, the eyes will get deeper, and there'll be pretty deep cuts at the sides of the nose. Most of the features are just about relative depth, but there's one place where something is actually stacked on top of something else: where the cheekbone runs over the top of the jaw. Be careful at first to leave enough uncarved material there, so that later you have enough room to get the jawbone tucked under the cheekbone.

At first you may want to make several passes through the following steps, carving away only a little at a time, and gradually reaching the full depth in all your cuts. Then as you gain confidence, you'll be able to cut to the full depth right away, blow right throw the steps and toss this book out the window. But you shouldn't do that. Use it to line a birdcage or something, okay?

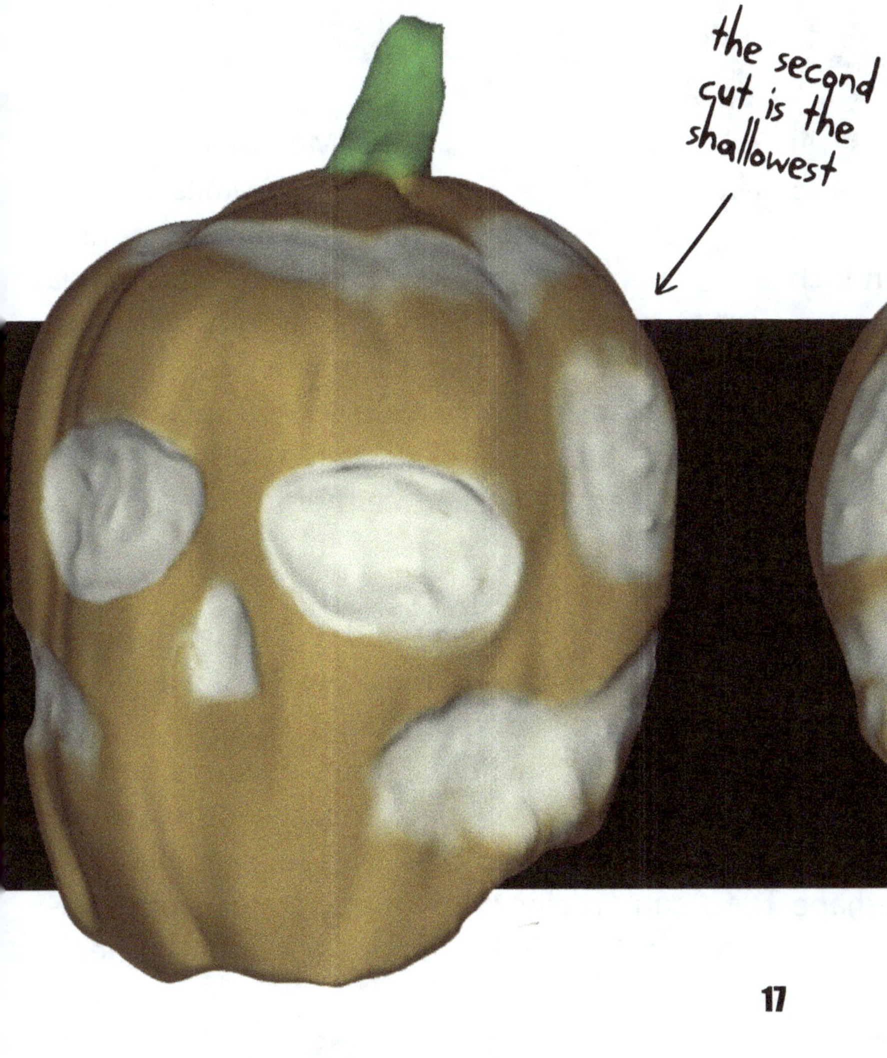

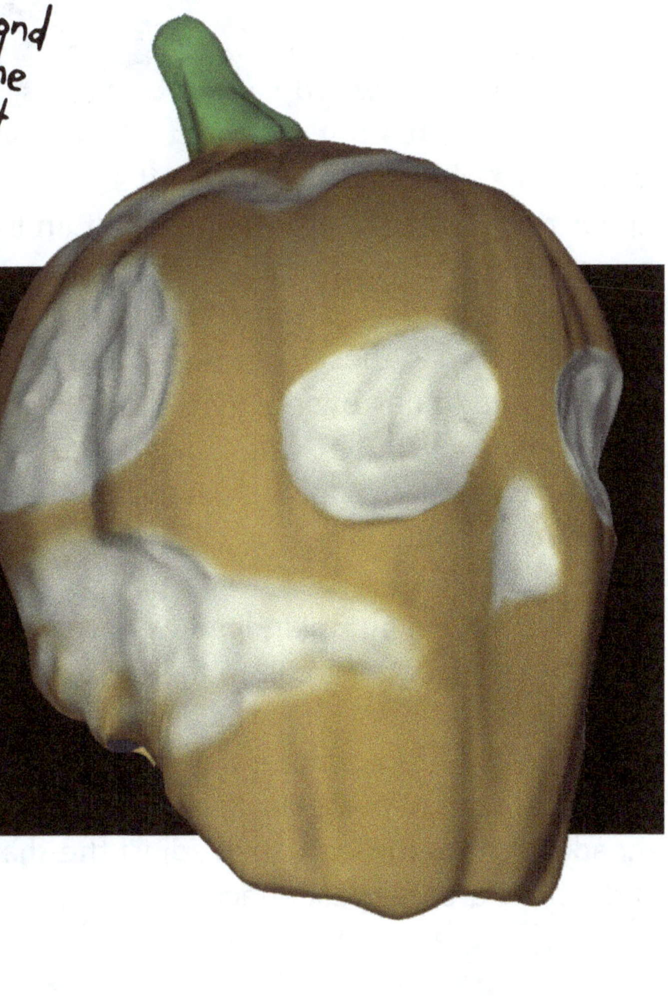

Step 4. Scooping the sockets

Keep looking at your references as you go, starting shallow (because there's no "undo" button). What you're scooping is called the "orbit," which is kind of a weird name if you ask me. It's not a perfect sphere like the eyeball is, and it's bigger than the eyeball by almost half an inch in some spots to allow wiggle room for the various muscles, nerves and tendons in charge of eyeball-related duties. The back of the orbit has a couple of narrow openings for the optic nerves and such, but it's basically a deep, bowl-like structure. An eyebowl, if you will. Will you? Perhaps you shouldn't.

Of course here in pumpkin-land we rarely have enough depth for true realism there. So I like to start the deep cut for the orbit as though it will end up in a perfect sphere, but there's a point where I run out of pumpkin. So at that point I go ahead and poke through, then adjust the shape of the hole later for best effect.

I usually try to resist the temptation to make mean-looking eyes, because it feels like a gimmick. Mean-looking people don't have skulls that are any meaner-looking than nice people, right? Of course there are times when mean eye sockets really can look convincing and cool. Ray Harryhausen's skeletons in Jason and the Argonauts looked super-mean and I'm still scared of them. So again, it's your call; just another rule to either follow or break.

Step 4a. Scalping

I like to keep checking and changing the overall shape of the skull as I go, always looking at it from different angles. I didn't want to call this a whole "step" because it happens all along, in between the other steps, but eye-scooping time is about as early as you can really think about cranial modification, so I figured I should talk about it here.

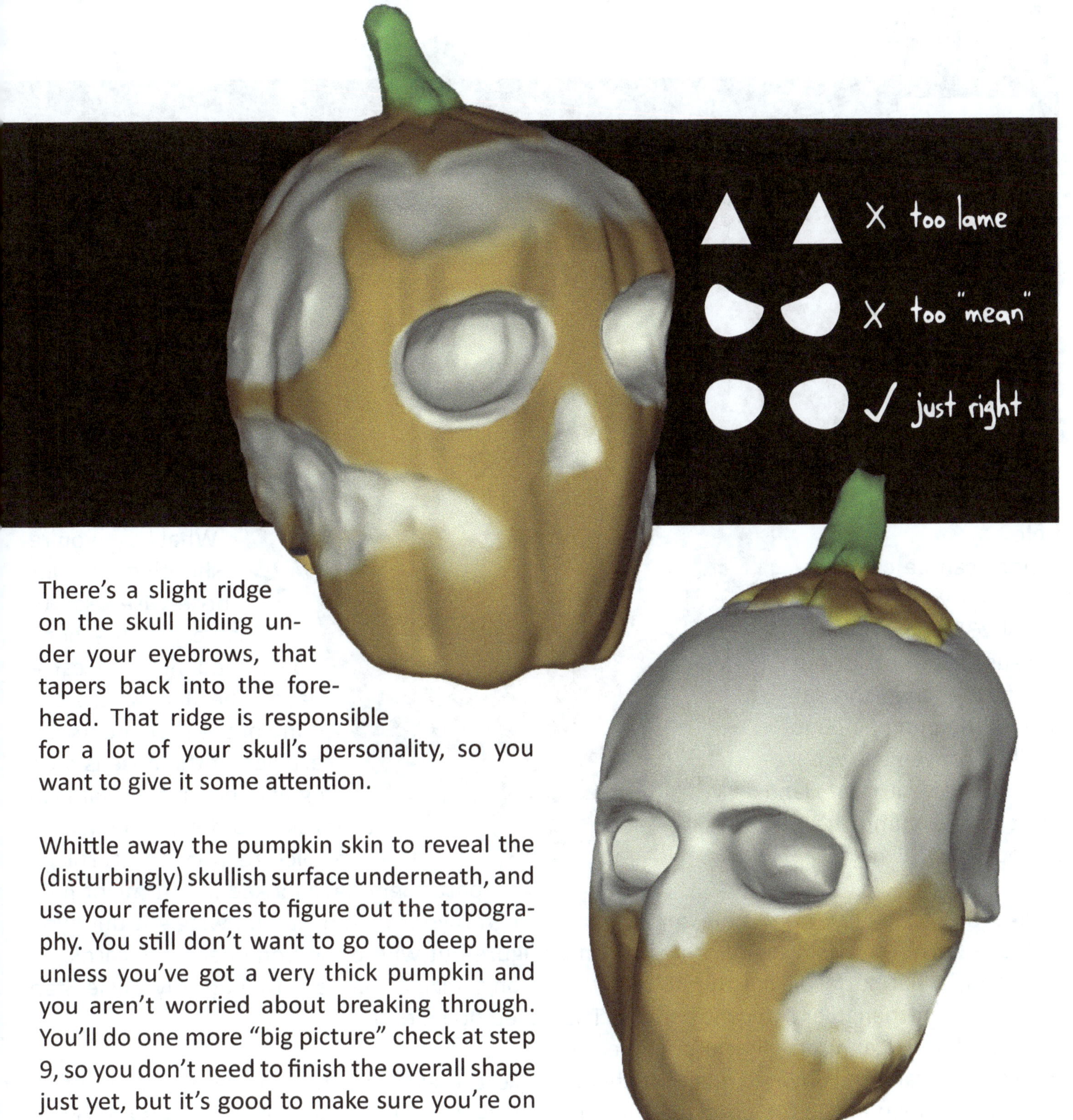

There's a slight ridge on the skull hiding under your eyebrows, that tapers back into the forehead. That ridge is responsible for a lot of your skull's personality, so you want to give it some attention.

Whittle away the pumpkin skin to reveal the (disturbingly) skullish surface underneath, and use your references to figure out the topography. You still don't want to go too deep here unless you've got a very thick pumpkin and you aren't worried about breaking through. You'll do one more "big picture" check at step 9, so you don't need to finish the overall shape just yet, but it's good to make sure you're on the right track.

It's nice to leave enough of the pumpkin skin showing so that folks who don't know for sure whether it's a pumpkin can figure it out without you telling them. You can undercut the skin a bit so it looks like the skull is wearing some kind of a weird pumpkin beanie hat or a dumb hairdo. Or make the pumpkin-to-bone transi- tion more organic, so it looks like the pumpkin is fused to the skull, or is in the middle of some kind of really messed-up metamorphosis. The point is, it's better to make a decision about that transition than to just let it happen accidentally.

Step 5. Picking your nose hole

A nose can be challenging when you're making a fleshy 3D pumpkin face, because it can't stick out any farther than the surface of the pumpkin. But a skull is conveniently nose-less, so the nasal cavity lands right at the pumpkin's outer surface.

Unlike the triangular nose hole on a jack-o'lantern, the nasal cavity of a skull isn't sitting on a flat surface—it's the hole at the top of a semi-triangular "volcano" shape. The sides of that volcano taper back to where the eye sockets start, and down to meet the cheekbones. The slope at the top continues up into the bridge of the nose, and underneath there's a small, steep cut that bends sharply and flattens out into the "philtrum," which is where a more fleshy face might store its mustache. When you get that volcano shape right, lots of other parts fall together more smoothly.

What you're shooting for nose-wise, is to carve just the bony parts and not the cartilage. The line where the bone of the skull meets the cartilage of the nose is a bit irregular and isn't the same in every skull, but it can be helpful to try to picture what the cartilage part might have looked like. It might help to grab your own nose and wiggle it until you figure out where the bone becomes cartilage. Don't wiggle too hard though. My uncle Stan died doing that.

Like the eye sockets in a real skull, the nasal cavity goes in deep but not all the way through, and you're going to violate that rule if you're carving a pumpkin. But you shouldn't poke all the way through right away, because there's a risk of looking cartoonish. Start by making two shallow "pig nose" shapes, and dig deeper until it starts looking realistic (see below). There's a

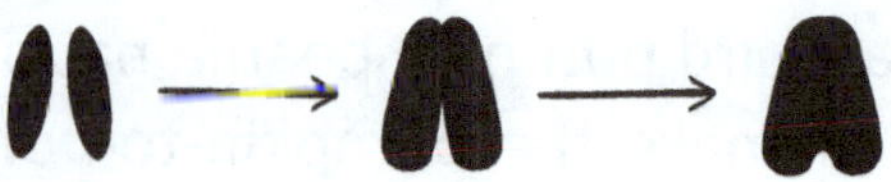

lot of variation in how up-side-down-heart-shaped that nasal cavity can be; sometimes it's like a round-ed triangle, sometimes there's almost total separation between the two halves. That means you get to decide. You get to choose your nose. Or pick it, as it were. See what I did there?

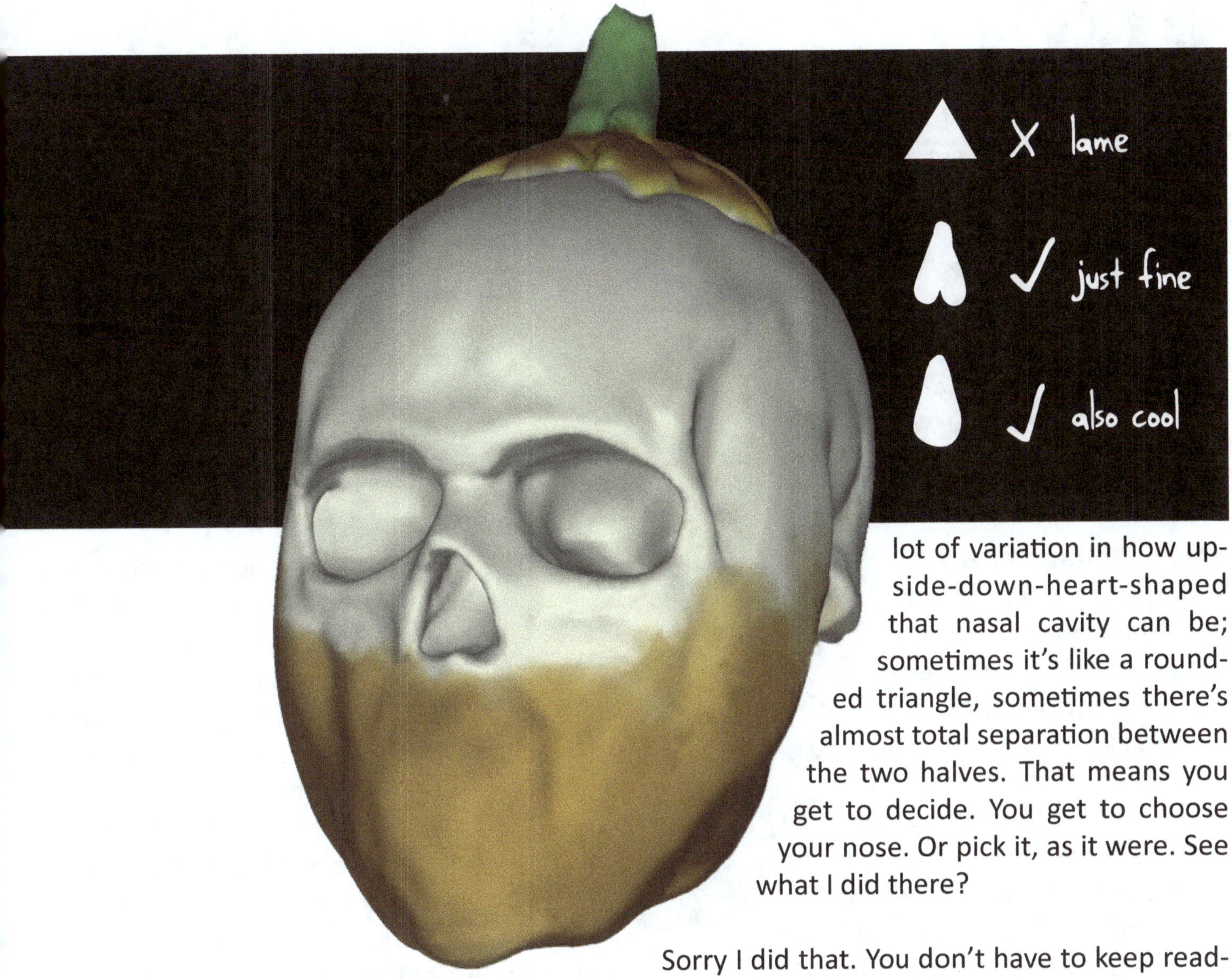

Sorry I did that. You don't have to keep read-ing if you don't want to.

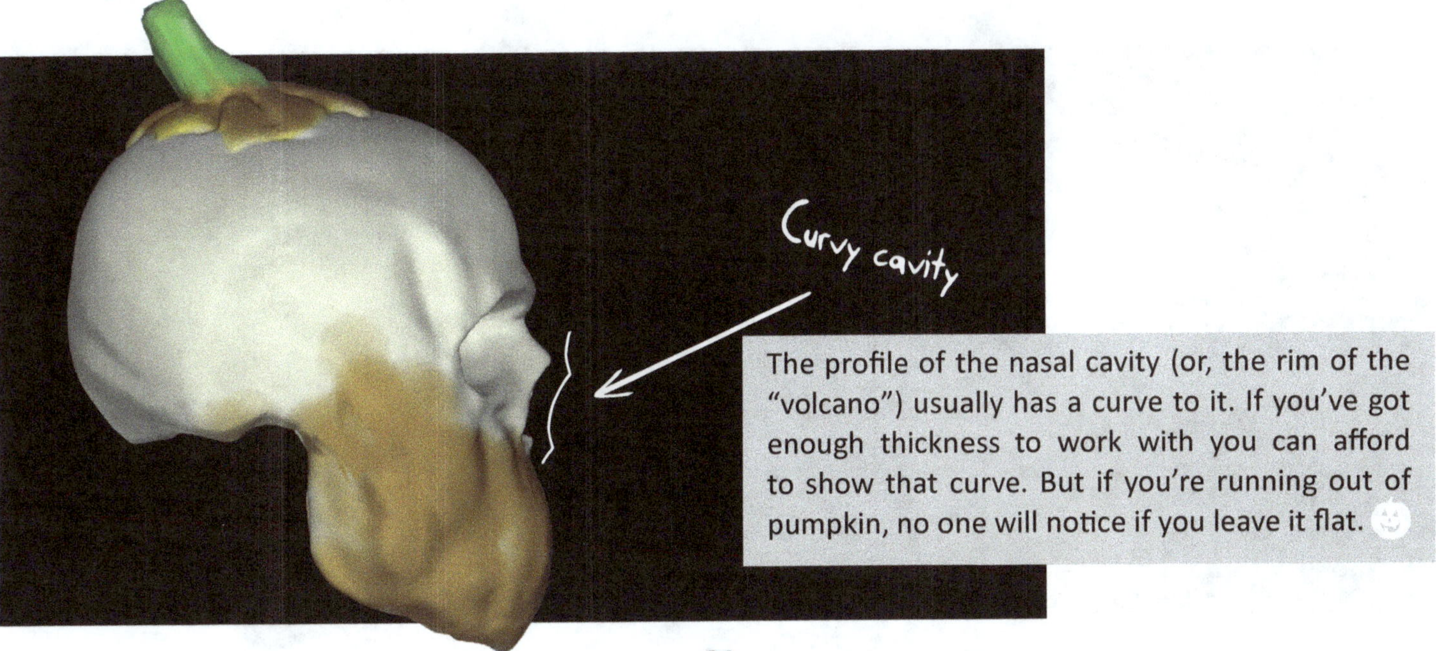

The profile of the nasal cavity (or, the rim of the "volcano") usually has a curve to it. If you've got enough thickness to work with you can afford to show that curve. But if you're running out of pumpkin, no one will notice if you leave it flat.

STEP 6
GETTING CHEEKY

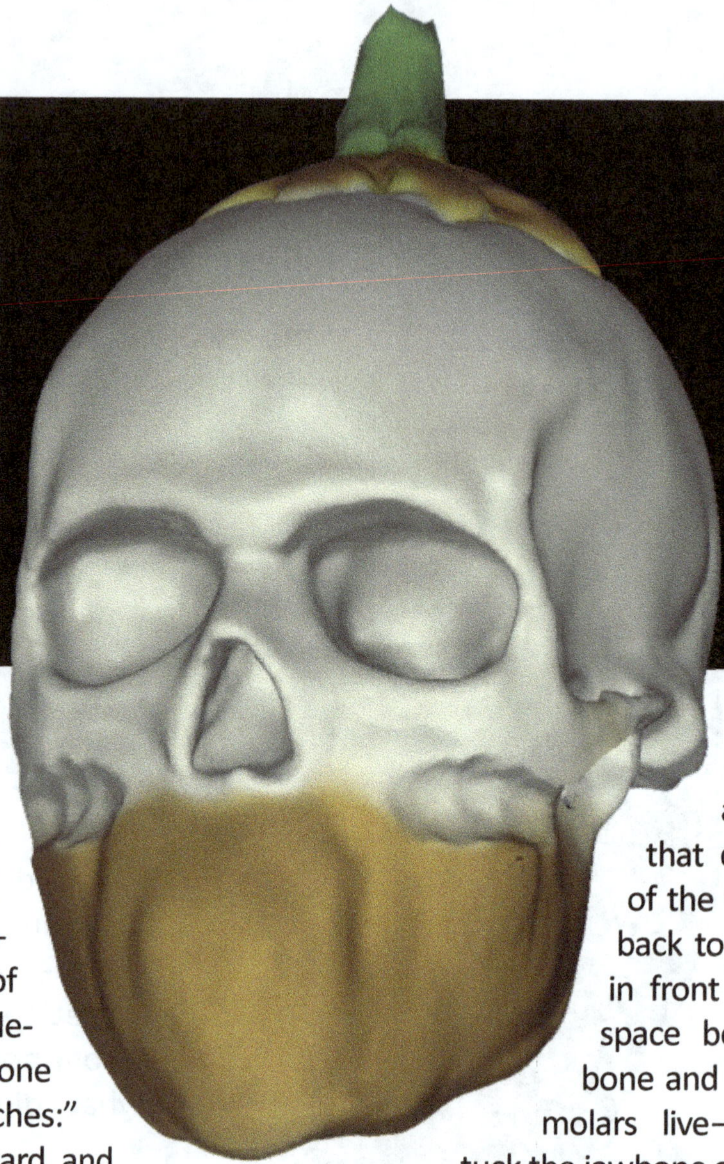

Step 6. Getting cheeky

Avoid going deep at first, but the cut under the cheekbone ends up being one of the deepest in the skull. The cheekbone should gradually ramp up to meet the side of the nose, then bulge out to define the actual cheek. That bone then splits into two "branches:" one thin branch curves upward and arcs around the eye sockets to define the side of the temple. The larger "main" branch continues around the side of the skull in a nearly straight line that defines the bottom of the temple, then tapers back to meet the skull just in front of the ear. There's space between the cheekbone and the spot where the molars live—enough space to tuck the jawbone and the muscles that make it go. But it's best not to cut too deeply there until you're done with the jaw (step 8).

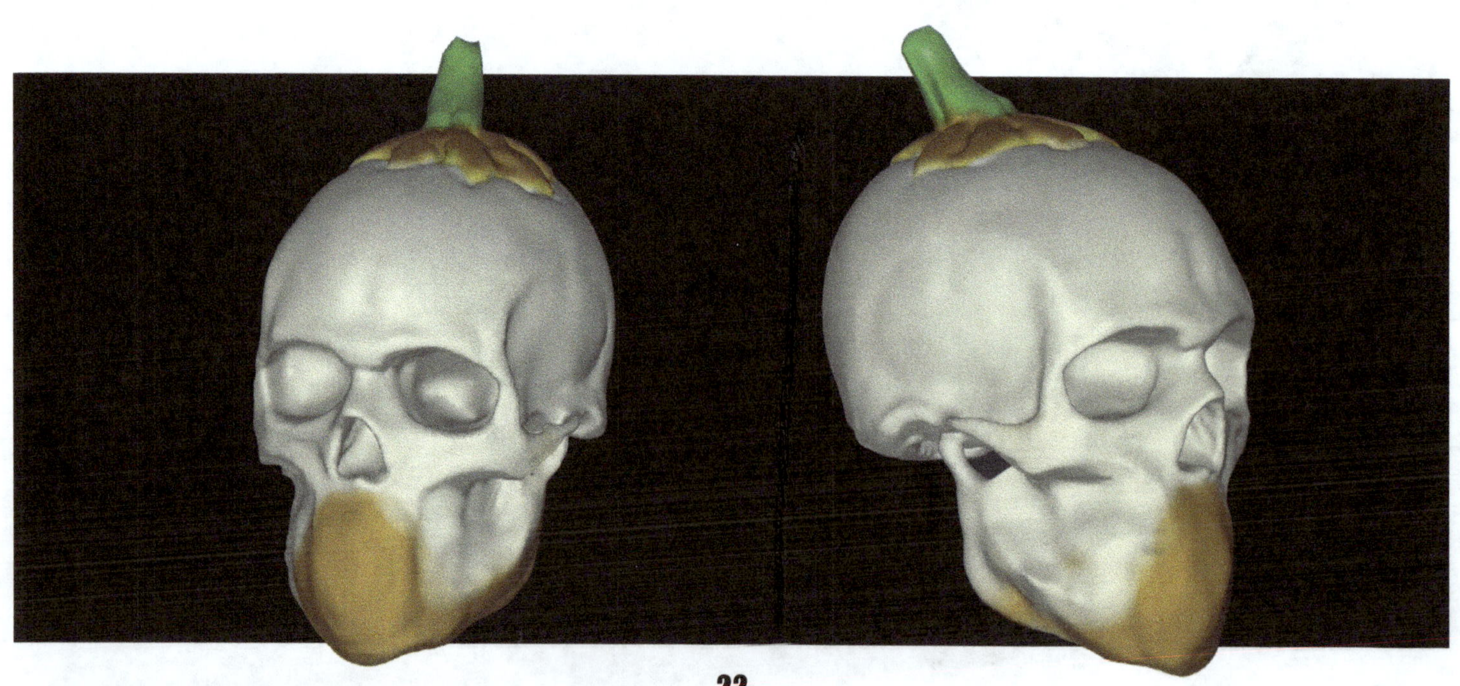

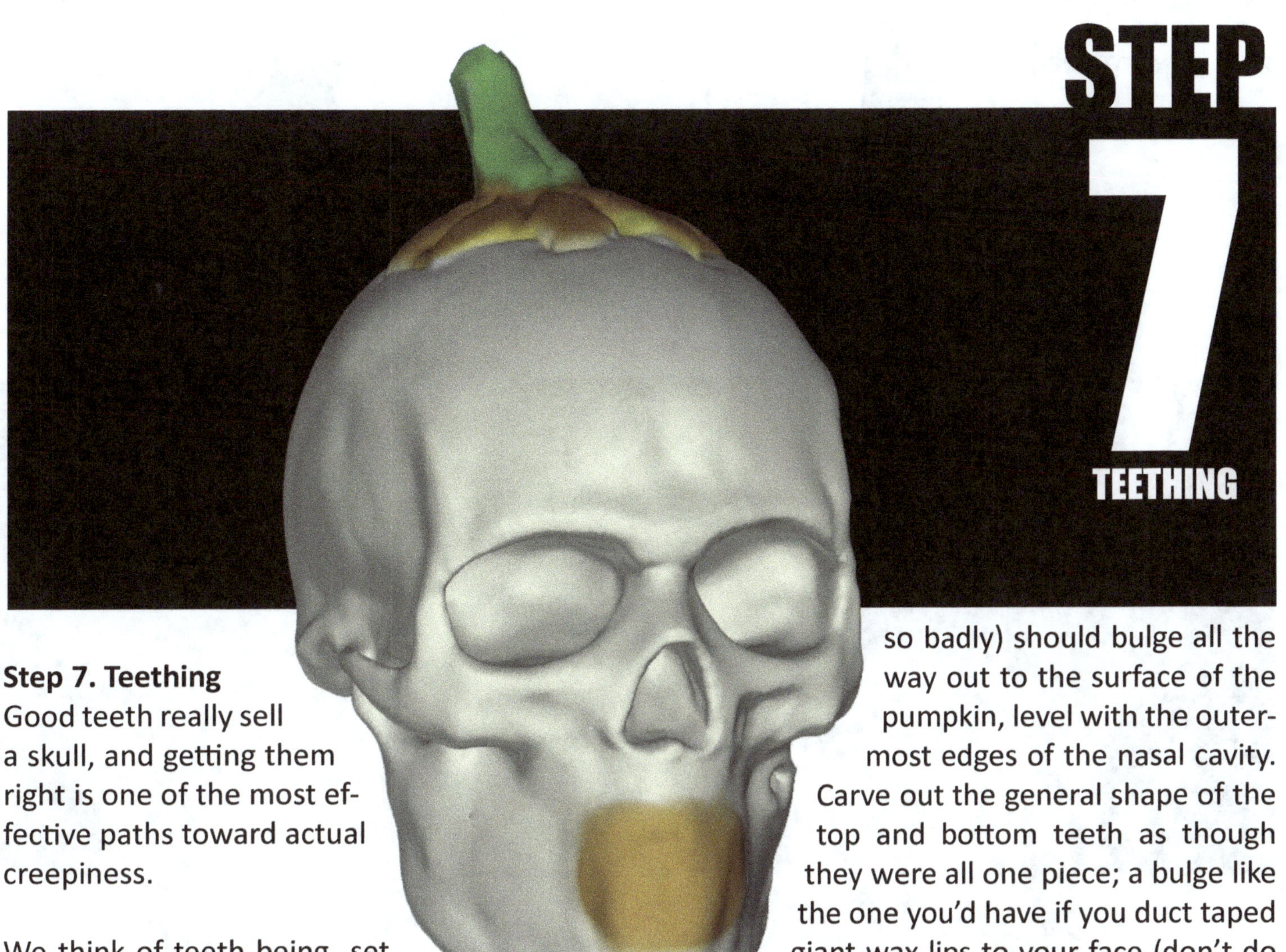

Step 7. Teething

Good teeth really sell a skull, and getting them right is one of the most effective paths toward actual creepiness.

We think of teeth being set back into our heads, but when you look at a skull you see that the teeth actually bulge forward. In fact, the outermost point of your pumpkin's teeth (including the two front ones that those silly children in that weird Christmas song want so badly) should bulge all the way out to the surface of the pumpkin, level with the outermost edges of the nasal cavity. Carve out the general shape of the top and bottom teeth as though they were all one piece; a bulge like the one you'd have if you duct taped giant wax lips to your face (don't do that, just see the image below). That bulge continues around the side, tapering back where the molars will end up under the cheekbone. Once that general shape looks right, you can move on to make the individual teeth.

more teeth on page 24

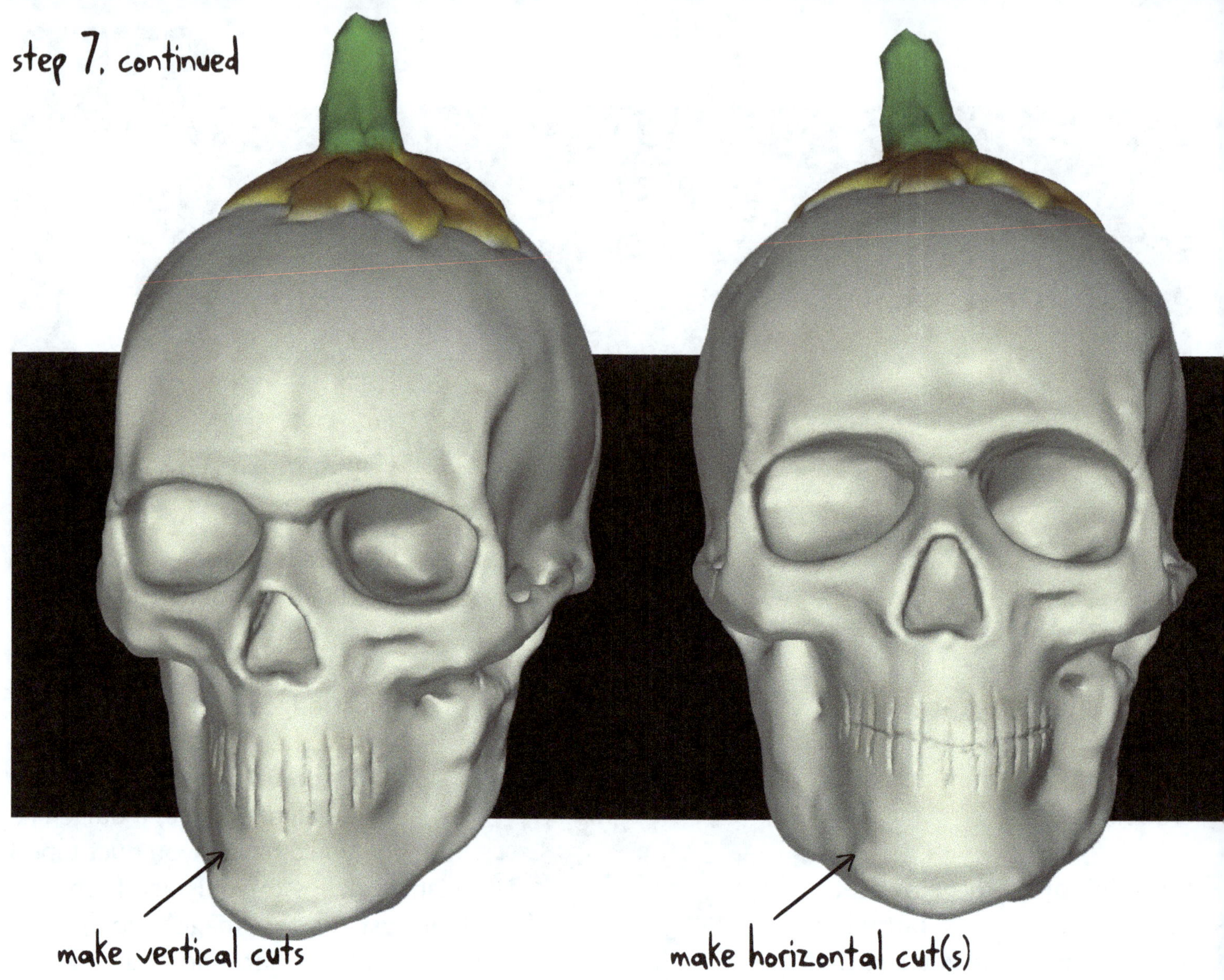

This is a place where you should decide how much you want to worry about realism. You can really get obsessive and make each tooth like it really is, and that will look great. But this is a spot where not too many people will notice if you fudge a bit, just making plausible tooth-like shapes instead of exact replicas.

Using a right-angle chisel, start with horizontal vertical lines between each tooth. You can either continue them all the way down across the bulge if you want the top and bottom teeth to line up, or do the top and bottom separately if you believe that the original owner of the skull didn't have access to quality orthodonture. Add a horizontal line where each tooth ends, taking care not to get too "smiley" (unless that's what you're going for). Add a little arc where each tooth meets the skull. Once that's done, it's easy to round out each tooth using other tools, and dig deeply along the spot where they meet the jaw for a very convincing look. The teeth

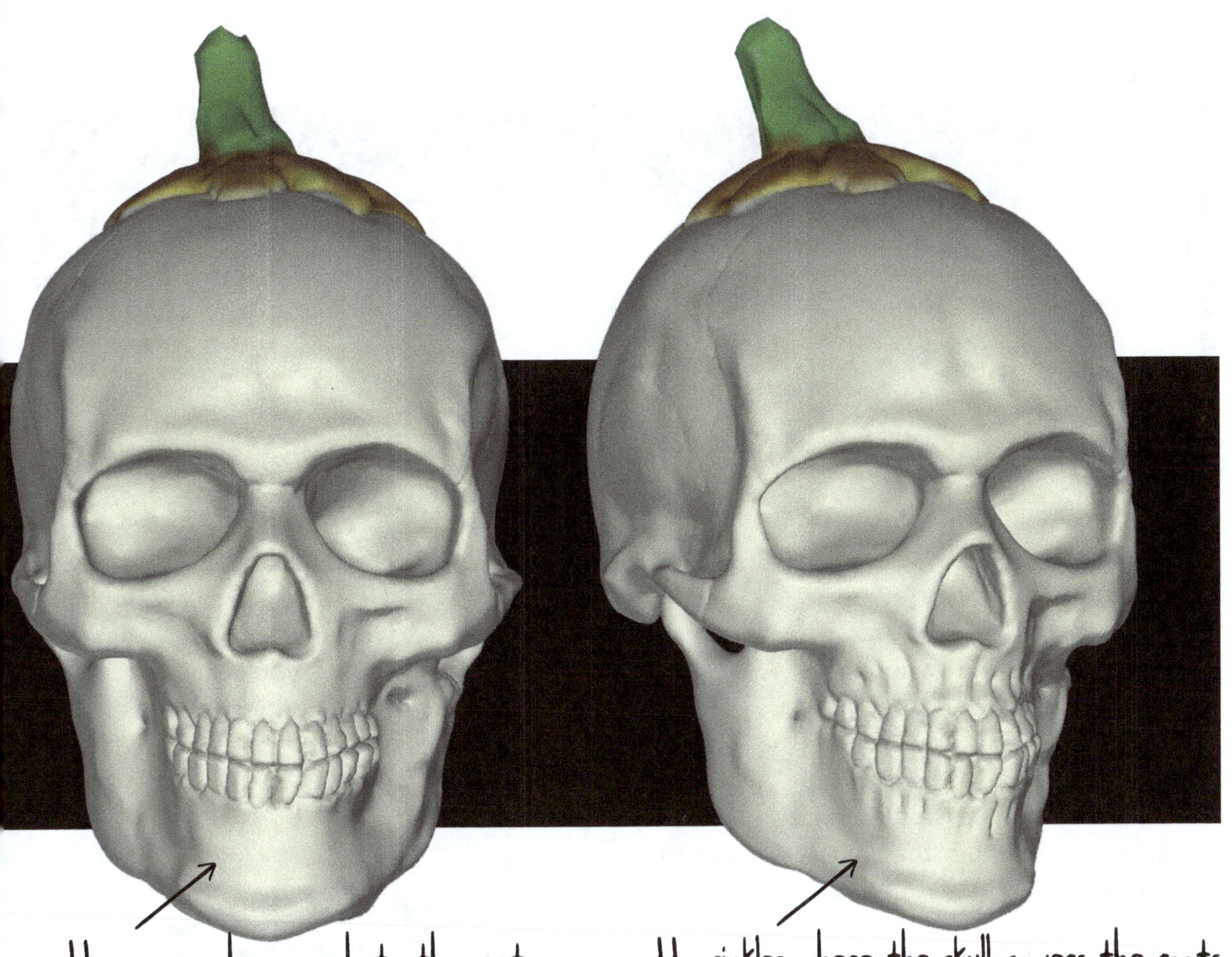

are a little longer than you think, and they narrow where they tuck into the jaw, making little gaps where you could floss them if you were so inclined. My particular favorite tool to use here is the sharp, curved cleanup tool. You can pretend you're a dentist if you want, I won't tell.

If you break a tooth, carve a big chunk out of it, or cut it out and leave a hole so it looks like it fell out. Or you can replace it with a new tooth made out of a chunk of pumpkin or carrot—just stick it in there using a (somewhat ironic) piece of toothpick. Or you can pull out one of your own teeth to use, but that seems like overkill.

The layer of bone at the base of the teeth is very thin and follows the shape of each tooth like a tiny, gross blanket, leaving little indentations in between. They're more pronounced in the mustache storage area, a bit less so at soul-patch level, but if you can capture the "dip" between the teeth, it can really help to sell the illusion.

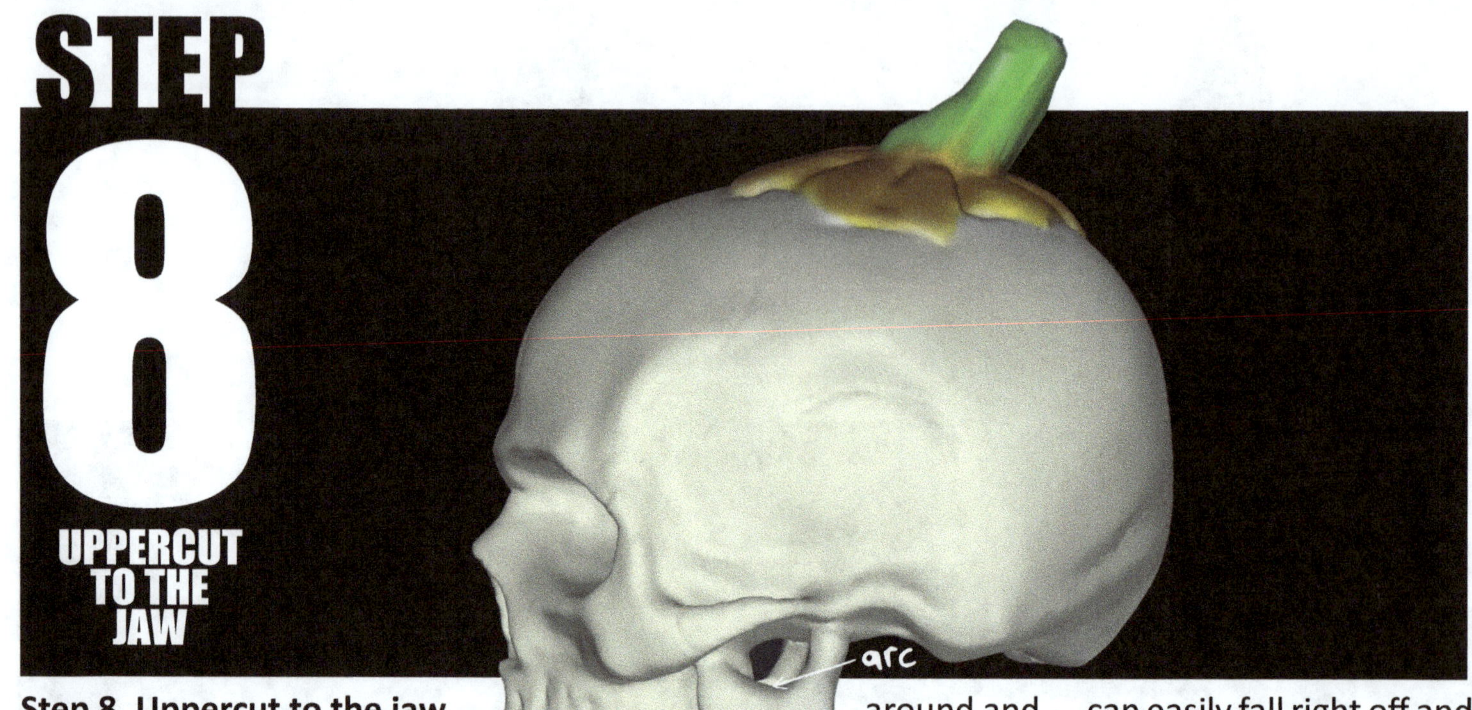

Step 8. Uppercut to the jaw
The jaw has an U-shaped arc shape at each end where it meets the skull. The back point of that arc is stuck under the horizontal part of the cheekbone, and the front point of the arc sits right under the highest point of the cheekbone.

Once you've defined the jawbone you can carve very deeply around it, then finish up cutting under the cheekbone. There's a lot of room under there because of a big jaw muscle called the "masseter" that runs underneath the cheekbone and connects to a wide, oval-shaped muscle at the temple called the "temporalis." Those muscles do the bulk of the work when it's time to chew something. Touch your temples while clenching your jaw and you can feel the muscles working together. If your pumpkin is thick enough, you can shoot for a realistic, bold undercut around the cheekbone. But if it's too thin, stay shallow and just try to show that the jawbone is overlapped by the cheekbone, by sharply defining your cuts.

Keep in mind that on a real skull (with no squishy bits attached), the jaw is just rattling around and can easily fall right off and get lost. So if the jawbone is giving you too much trouble, you'll still end up with a spooky skull if you just skip it entirely. Just make up a story about where it went, and you're covered.

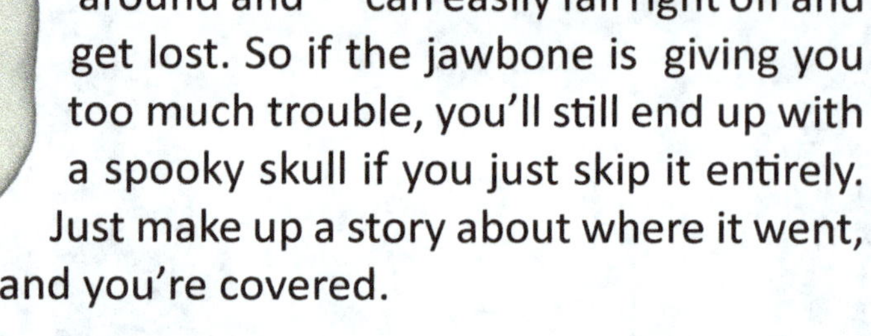

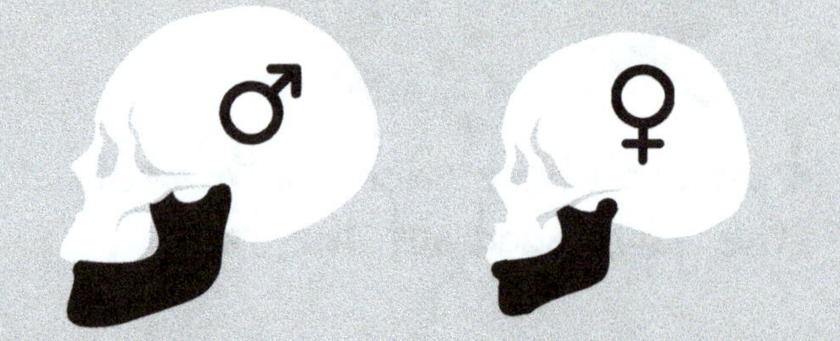

Anatomical note: A variation in the width of the jawbone is probably the most obvious difference between a male an female skull. If you pay attention to that, you'll see that almost every skull you can find, whether it's in a classroom or a Halloween store, is female.

There's a truly creepy history to where academic skeletons come from, and you should research that if you need more things to be disturbed about. Or if you're looking for a good premise for your scary novel: how about haunted classroom skeletons that come to life and start jaywalking or driving around without using their turn signal or ringing people's doorbells and hiding in the bushes giggling? Or I bet you can think of something scarier they should do. And when they make a movie out of your book, can I be in it? I'll work cheap, but I have some really strict riders in my contract regarding nacho cheese.

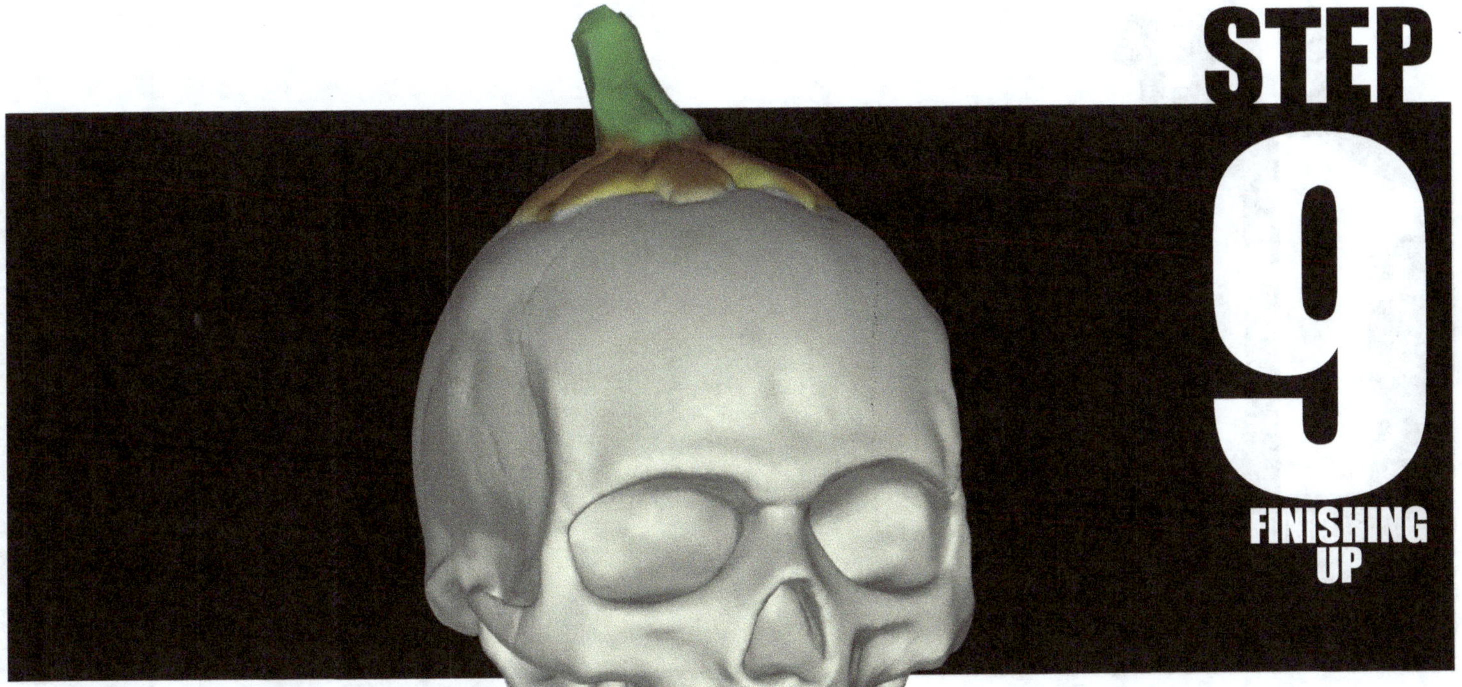

Step 9. Smooth it out, sew it up, and leave some bread-crumbs

If possible, do one more quick pass where you try to achieve the overall curve of the skull itself. You prob-ably won't get all the way there because a pear-shaped pumpkin is usually too spherical to hold a more egg-shaped brain, but you can always do some subtle adjustments that can help create the illusion of skullishness.

Note: I do this step late in the process because I want to save the thickness for the most import-ant details like the eyes and nose and teeth; it's still convincing if the overall shape ends up a bit too round.

Use your references and something sharp to locate and carve those squig-gly "sutures." It's a very easy ef-fect to achieve, and really adds to the creepy factor.

Stem-provements: If your pump-kin's stem was at the small end of your "pear" and you cut it off during step 1, consider cleaning all the pumpkin off of it and sticking it to the top of your pumpkin skull, using toothpicks and/or hot glue. Or if your pumpkin is stemless, you can often find a rotten pump-kin in a patch that has a cool stem that you can transplant. Or start holding on to the stem whenever you retire a pumpkin, and you'll build a collection you can use on your less stem-en-dowed creations. Or, look online. Apparently folks sell pumpkin stems. Who knew?

tinyurl.com/ybaf9vjc

Step 10. Show it off

My favorite way to display a pumpkin skull is to dangle it from a length of paracord - it swings ominously in the wind, and if you're lucky the air circulation will delay mold growth for a few extra days. To hang the skull I drill a hole in the top, usually right behind the stem so it tilts downward a bit when it's hanging, and I tie something to the cord that fits inside the skull. You need something in there that's big enough to provide support for the skull when it gets mushy. I've used a plastic ball (with a copyrighted name that rhymes with "skiffle"), sections of plastic bottles, and various configurations of duct tape. String the object through the hole you drilled, and your skull is ready to hang.

Luckily a good pumpkin skull looks increasingly awesome as it decays so there's no true expiration date, but you can prolong its life (or perhaps its death) by spraying all surfaces with vinegar or bleach water or bathroom cleaner, or by applying a layer of hand sanitizer. But then take some pictures, because mushification is inevitable no matter what you do.

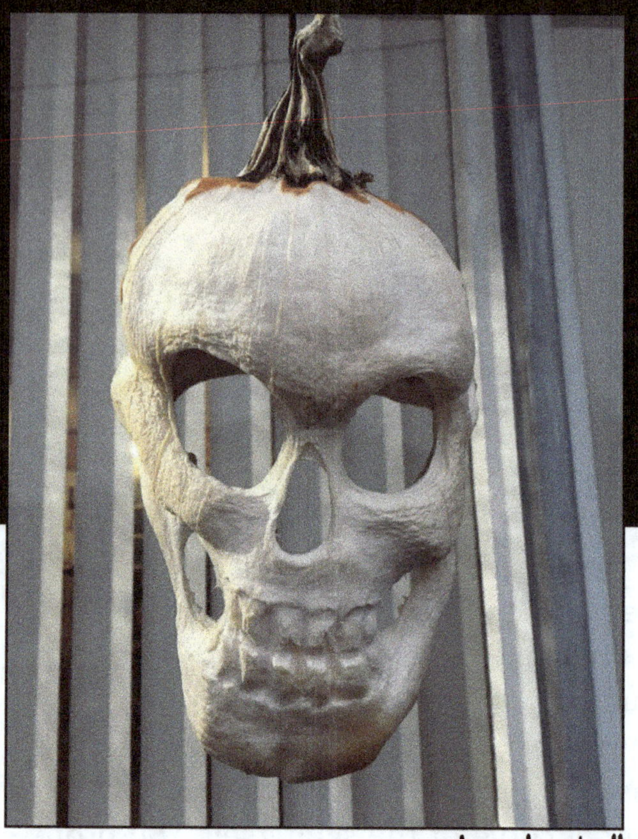

dangly skull

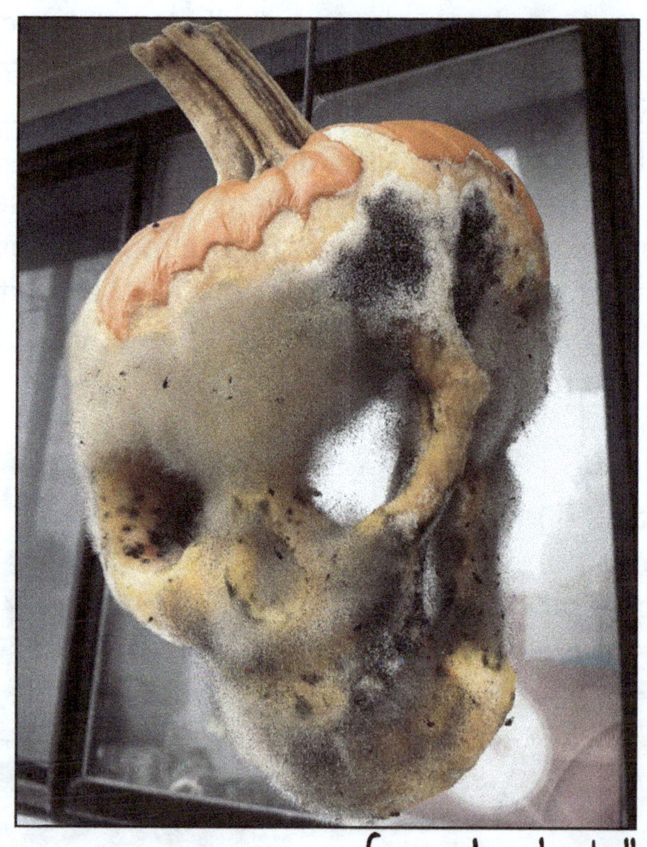

furry dangly skull

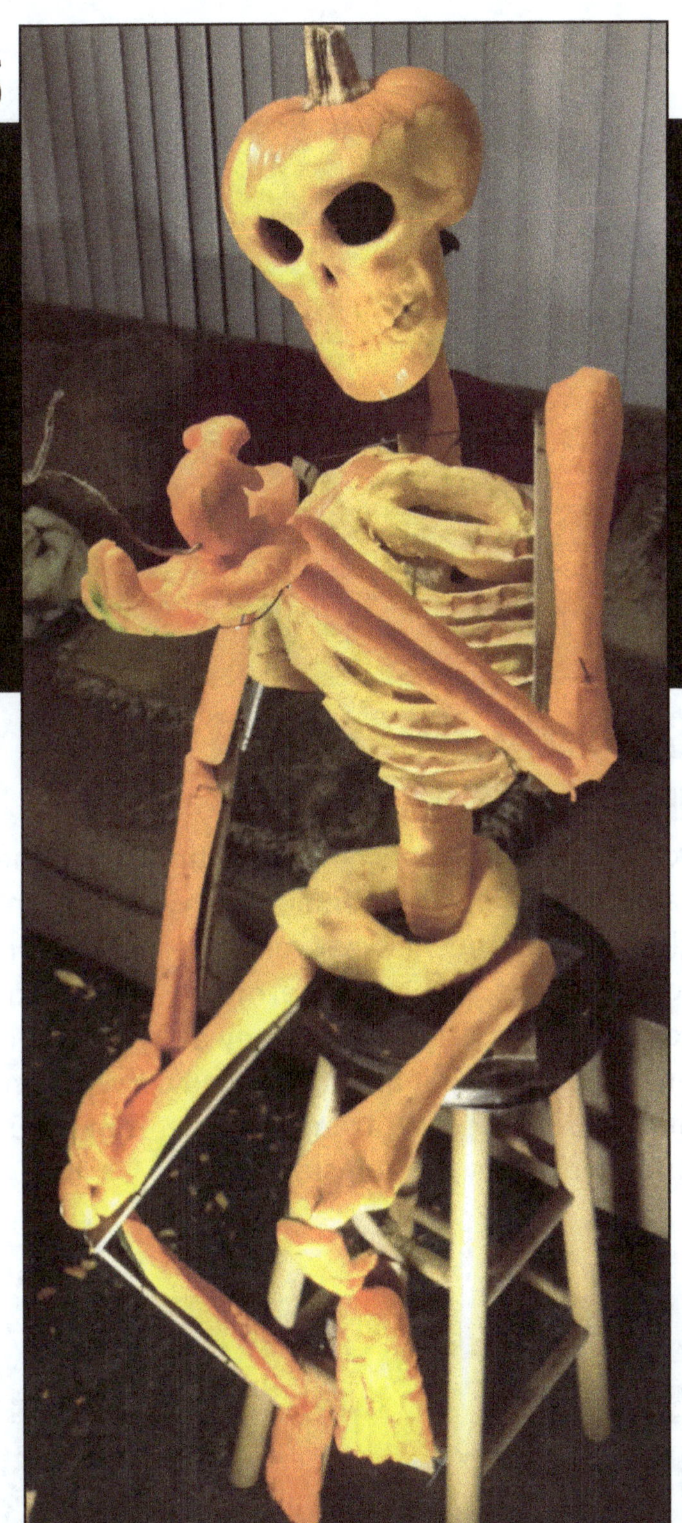

skull
danglers

Other display options include putting it on top of an entire skeleton made out of pumpkins, propping your skull up for table display, feeding it to a carnivorous monster you've made out of a bigger pumpkin, or just leaving it in the refrigerator to give everyone the willies. It's often a good idea to put something black inside where the guts used to be, to emphasize the eyes and nose and help it read from farther away.

It's tempting to light it from the inside like a jack-o'lantern or add LEDs to make the eyes glow, but I think that makes it look a few notches less realistic and therefore a few notches less creepy. I think it's best to find a place where it's dramatically lit from the outside, via porch light or a strategically-placed garden spotlight.

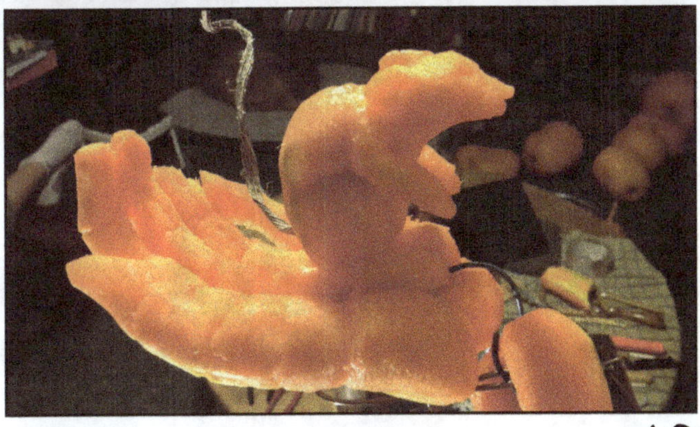

*more skeletons on page 43

STEP 11

Go back to step 1 and start again, because every time you do this it will get easier, and spookier. Then stop after a few, because come on, you have a life.

THERE IS NO STEP ELEVEN

Carving things out of non-pumpkins

You can attack many other victims with the same tools you use for pumpkin carving, including potatoes (sweet or otherwise), carrots, parsnips, turnips, watermelons, butternut squash, apples, and more. They all have different properties that affect how you carve them, and lifespans vary tremendously, but your pumpkins skills will transfer directly.

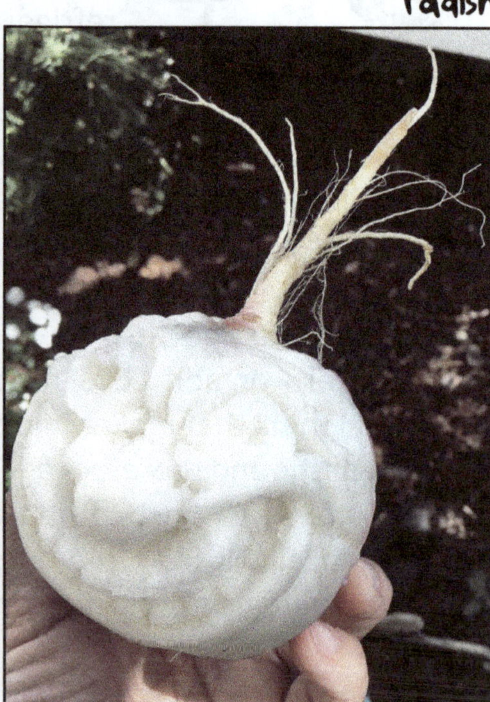

watermelon

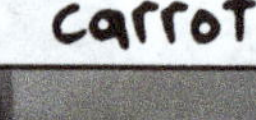

butternut squash

carrot

radish

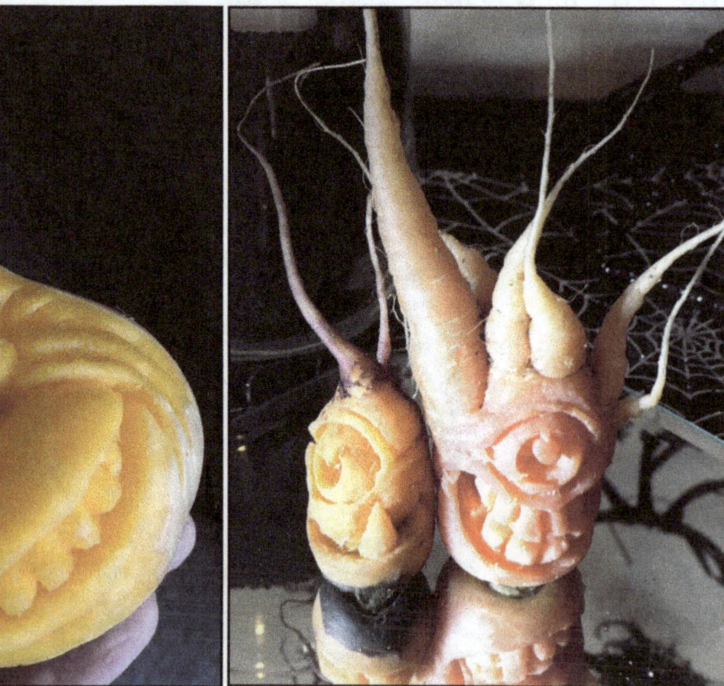

I would be remiss here if I didn't sing the praises of my favorite non-pump-kin item - it's a squash called the **Long of Naples**, or **Naples Long**. It's easy to find if you live in my home-town—just head out to Organic Mat-ters Ranch (6821 Myrtle Ave., Eure-ka, CA) during pumpkin season—but you might have trouble finding them where you live. From the outside they look like an enormous zucchi-ni, but inside their flesh is a deep reddish-orange, and is almost solid. This makes them a great choice if you need to carve a life-sized human arm or a bunch of giant spider legs or a stack of skulls and snakes. I've carved all of these and more out of Naples Longs, and I always make sure I add a few to my pile of victims each season.

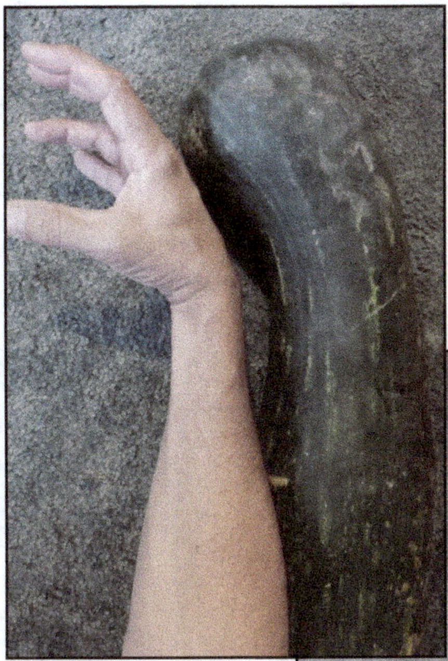

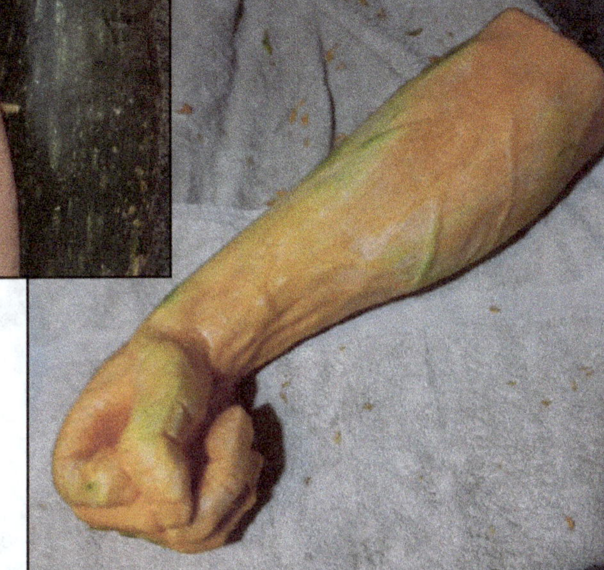

crab with snack, 2015

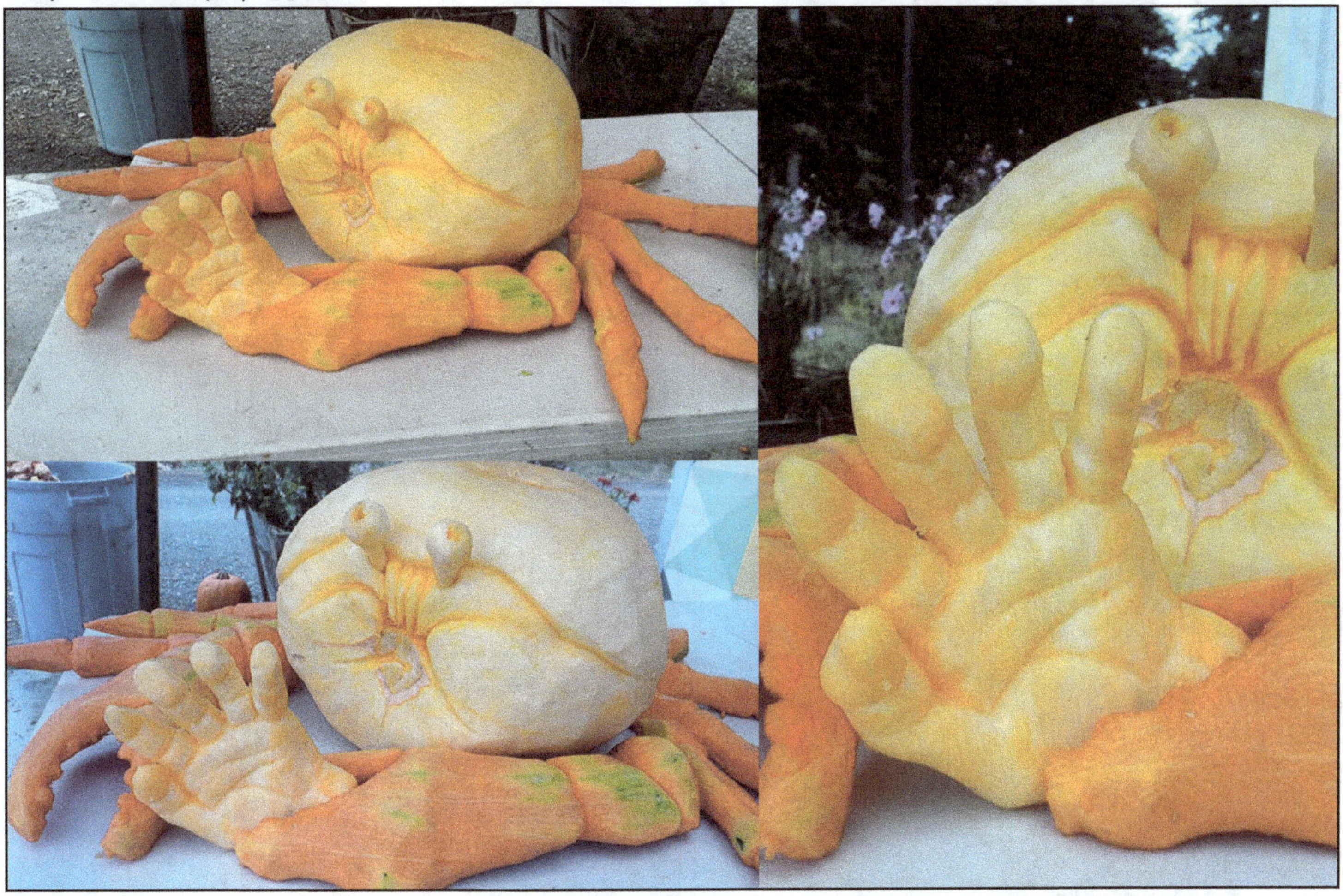

Carving things out of sand

Your pumpkin-carving skills will also translate to sand, but you'll have to collect a different assortment of tools and read sandy books and practice a lot. If you're interested, a great place to start is with Lucinda Wierenga at **sandyfeet.com**.

literal zoology, 2009: horse fly, etc... get it?!

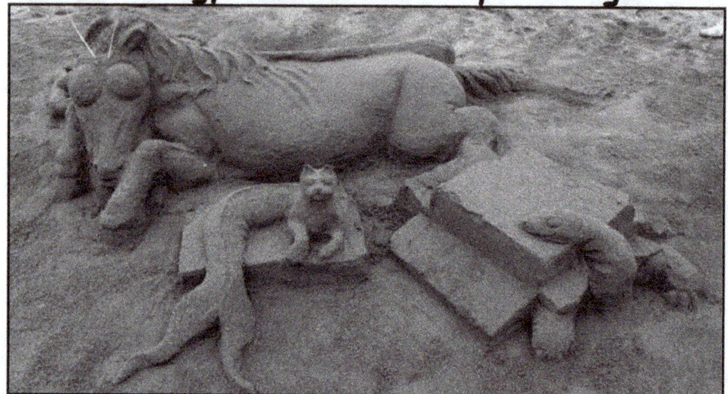

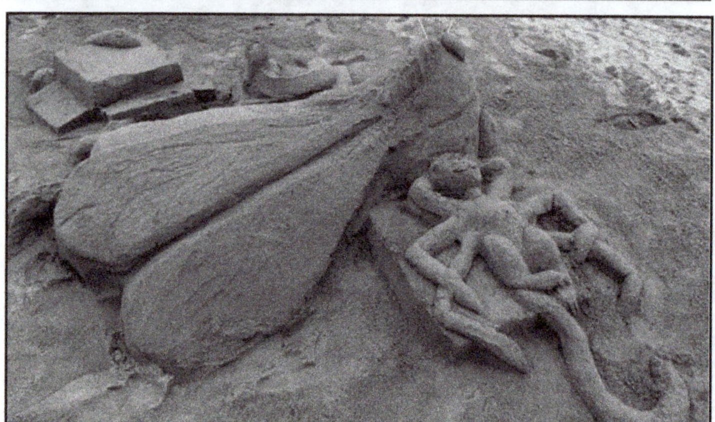

croctopus, 2016: teeth & tentacles

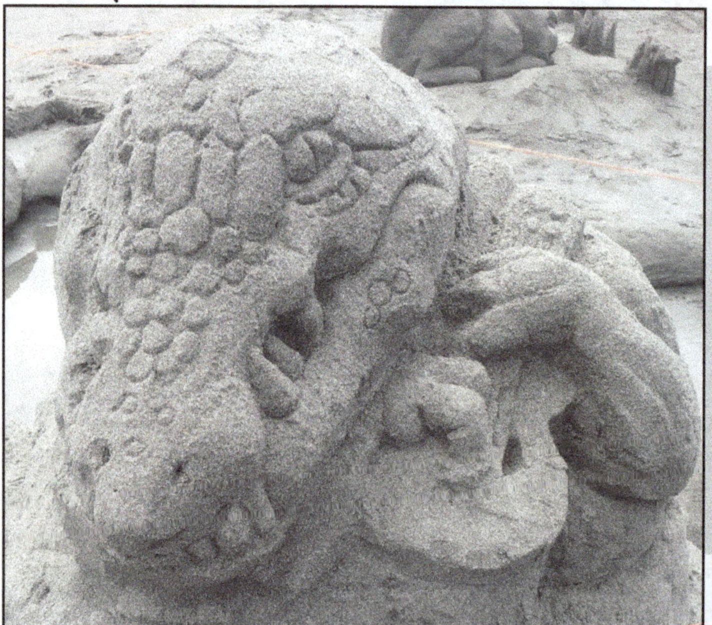

hazards of sunbathing, 2007

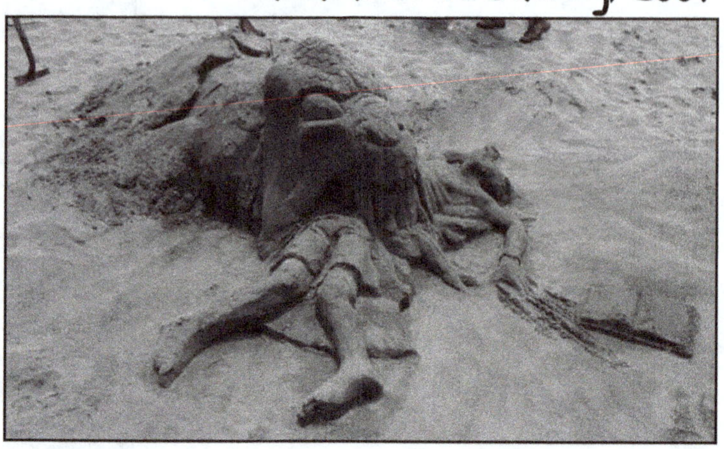

bad donut, 2011

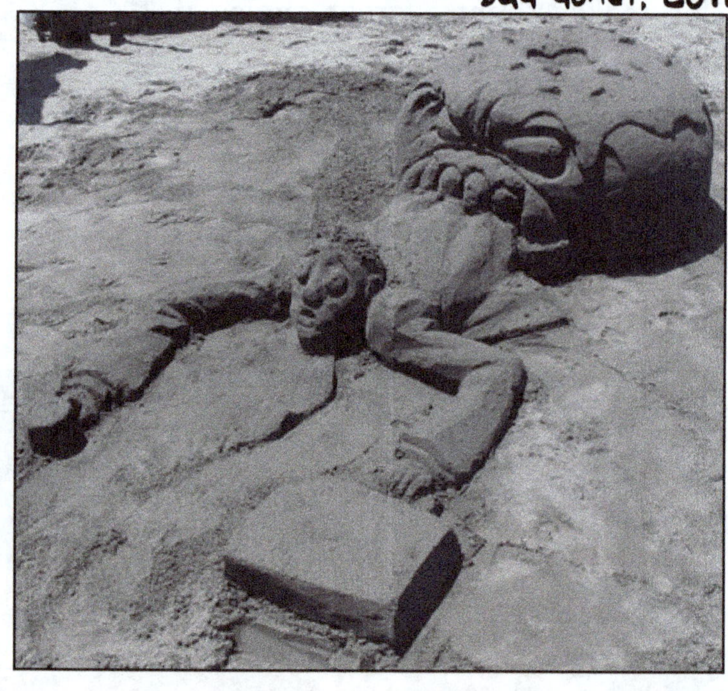

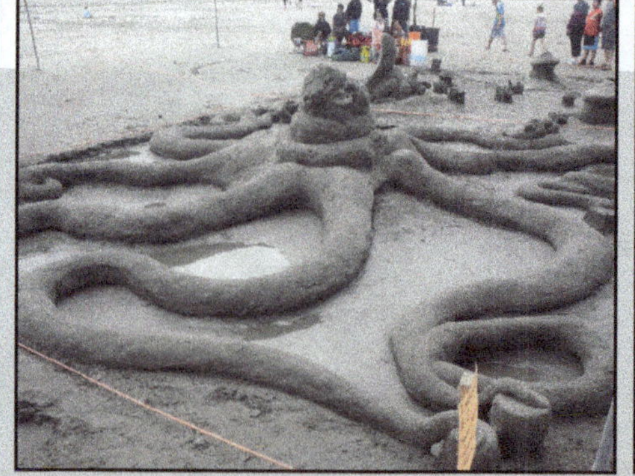

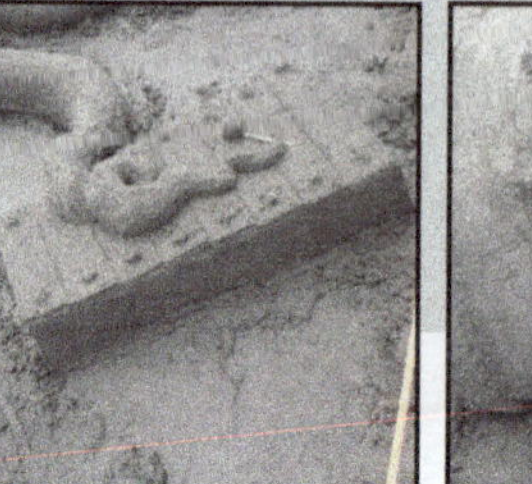

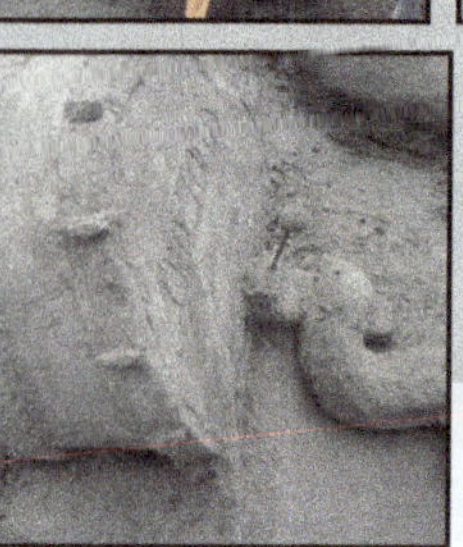

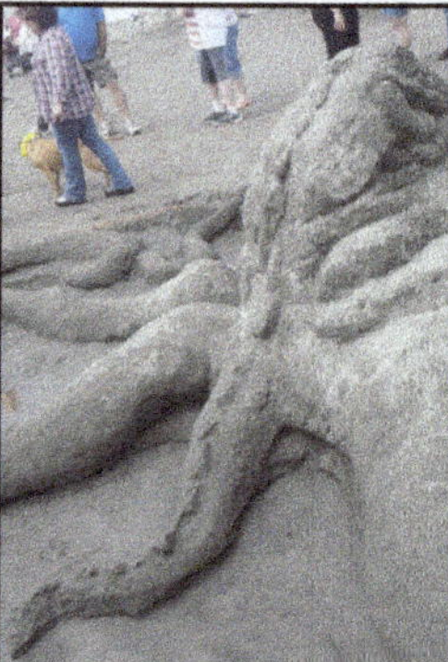

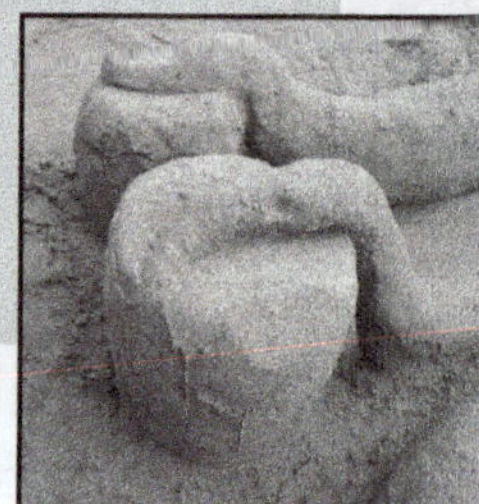

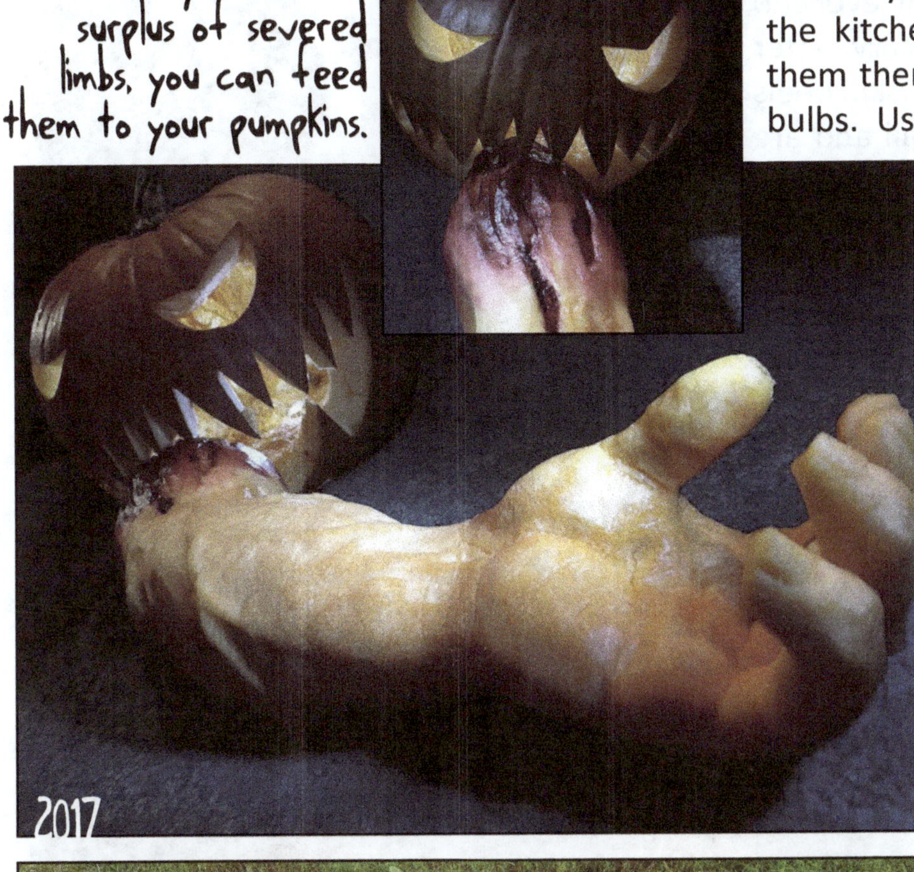

2017

Candle placement

Carefully place your candles in the drawer in the kitchen by the coffee maker and leave them there. The same goes for incandescent bulbs. Use LEDs instead! I think 3D carved pumpkins look best when lit from the outside with light aimed so that the shadows are distinct. But in cases where there's a need for internal lighting (like the carnivorous jack-o'lantern at left), use LEDs whenever possible, because they generate far less heat. And heat fosters the growth of mold and bacteria and all kinds of creepy crawlies, which will accelerate the evolution into mush.

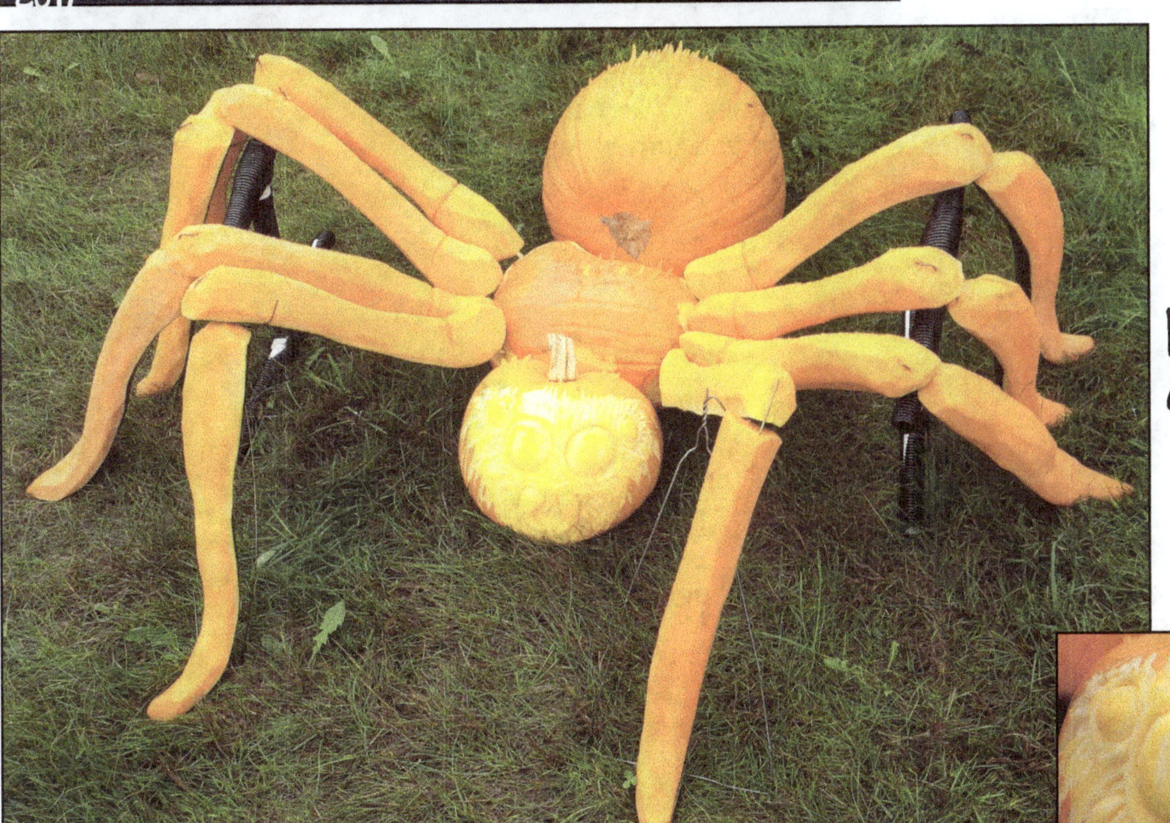

lawn spider, 2016

warning: do not do a web image search for "spider faces." it's really scary.

Avocado pits:
tiny pumpkins

Another item to consider is the lowly avocado pit: they're small, but pretty easy to carve after sitting for a few days (so their papery skin peels off easily). They'll hold a lot of detail and are quite robust when completely dry, almost like hardwood. They have two hemispheres that want to break apart as they dry, so it's much easier to carve just one half than to try to make something out of the whole thing. But they should last forever. Add a little mineral oil for a nice reddish-brown finish and make a necklace or something.

Go ahead, I'll wait.

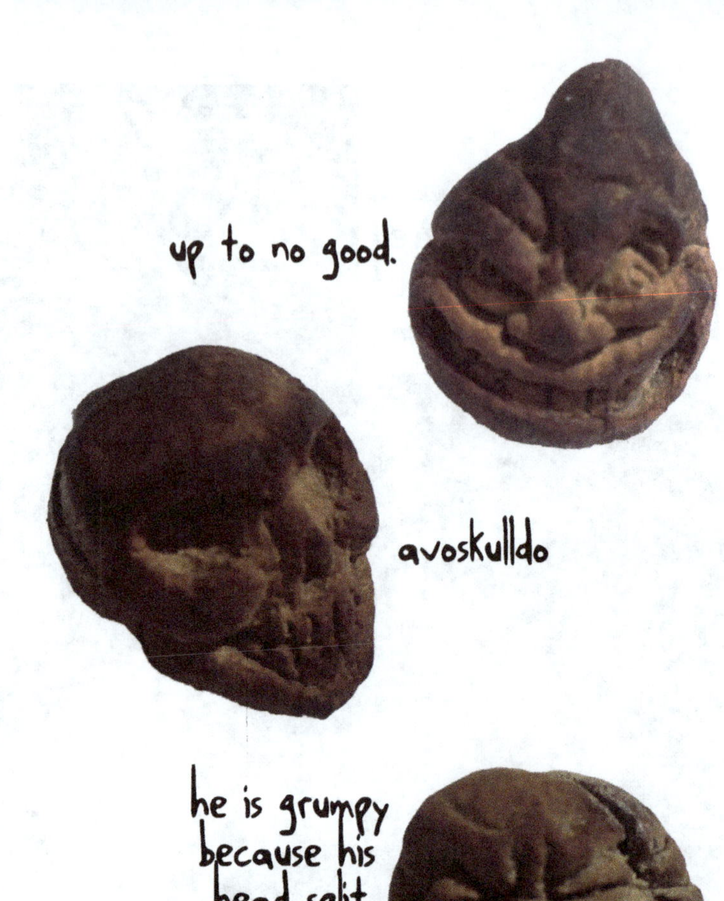

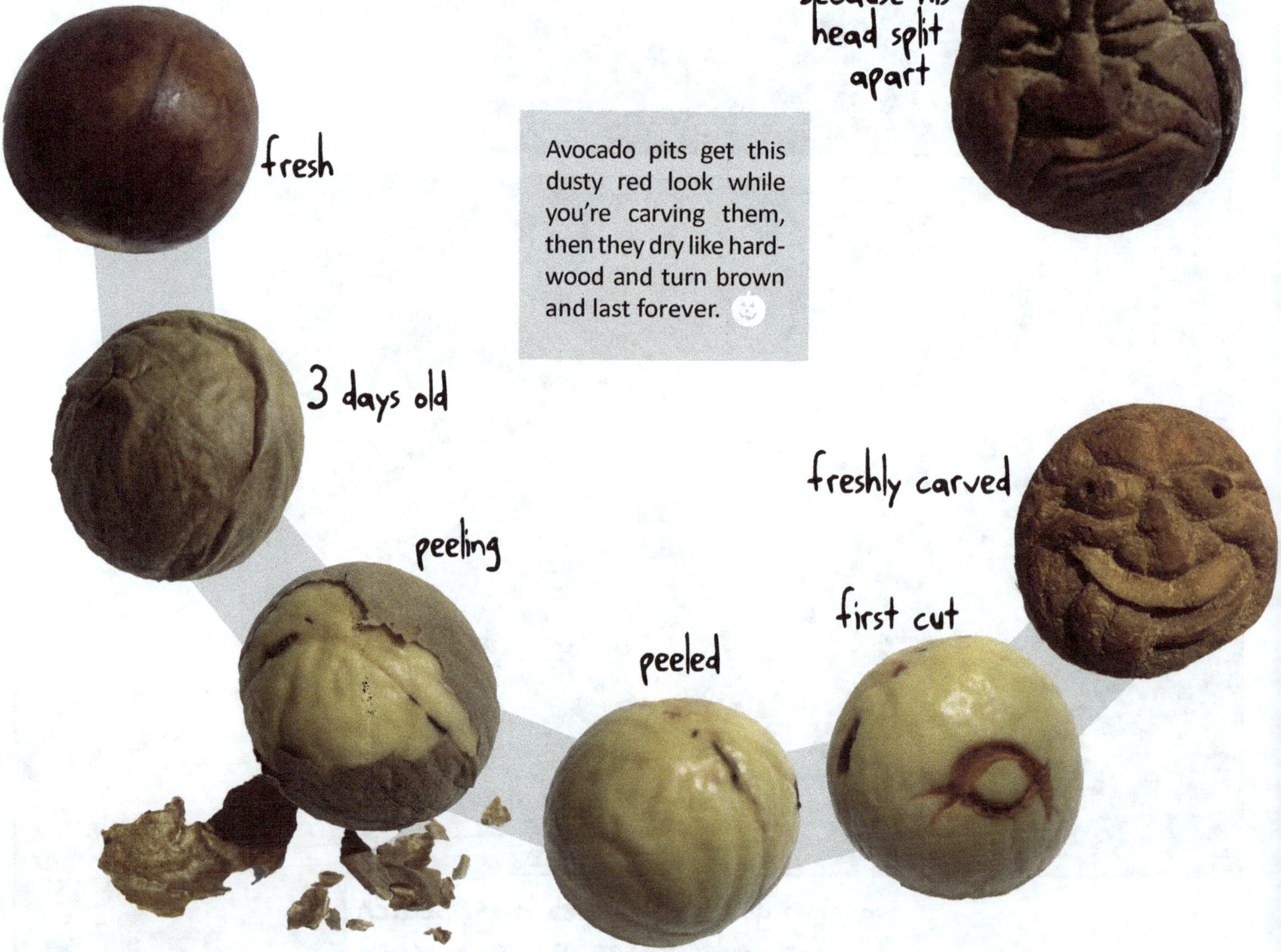

Avocado pits get this dusty red look while you're carving them, then they dry like hardwood and turn brown and last forever.

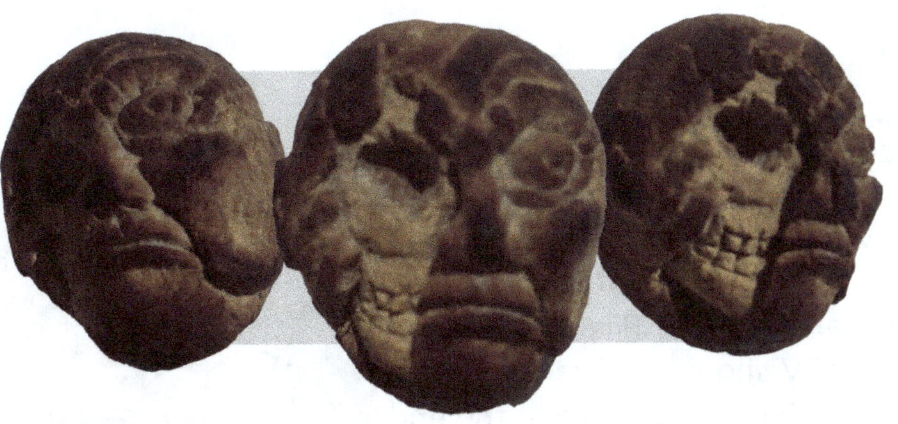

half his face is missing
and he looks grouchy.

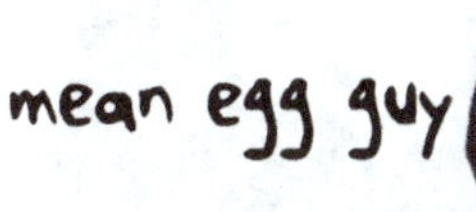

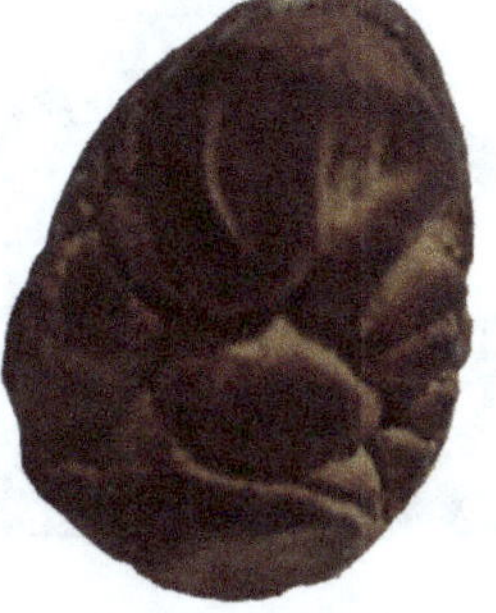

happy beard guy

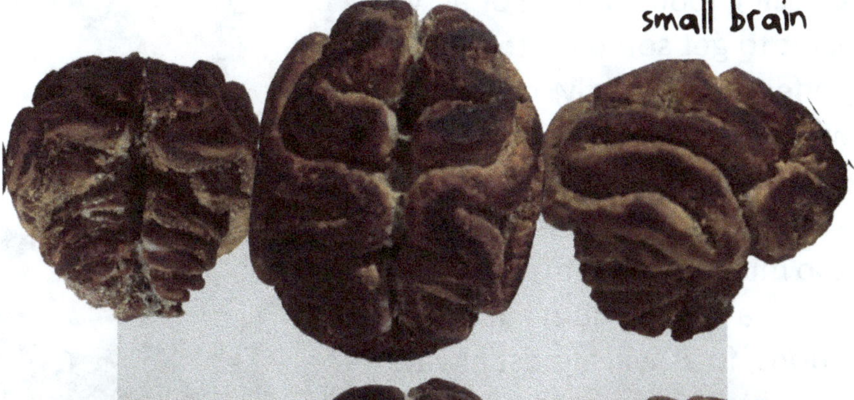

small brain

mean egg guy

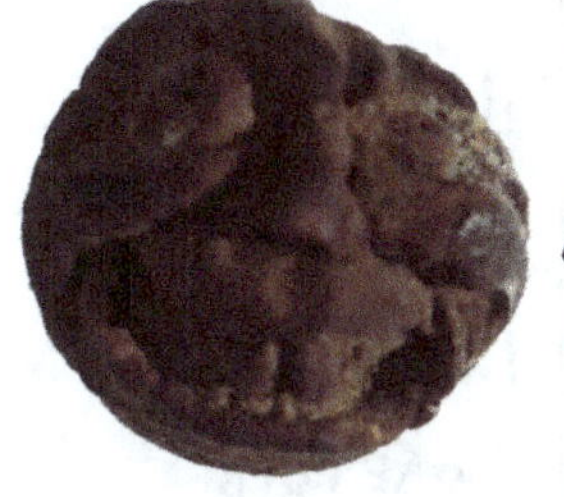

dave

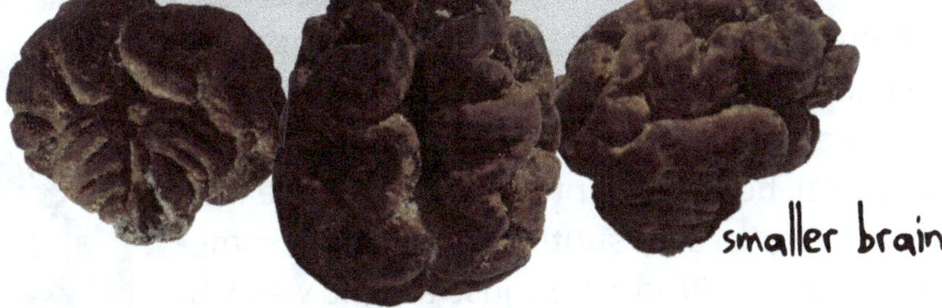

smaller brain

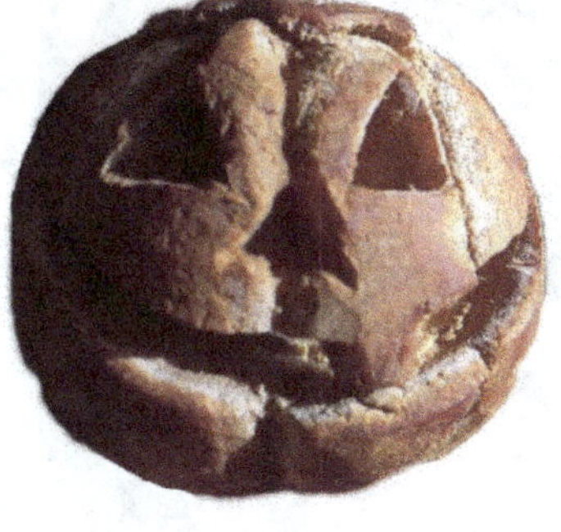

happy pumpkin

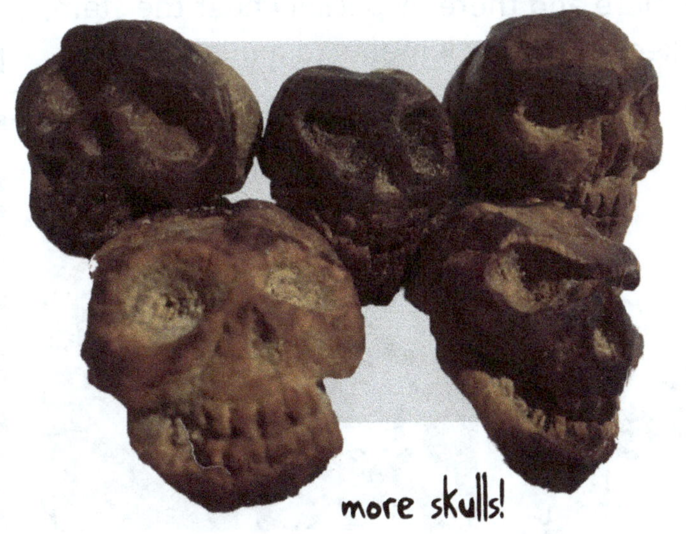

angry pumpkin

more skulls!

Painting pumpkins

When you're trying to make a pumpkin look like something else, or blend it in with other things like sugar and cake (like they do on that TV show that I talk about in the "Meet Mike" page at the end of this book that you shouldn't watch season 7 of), you can add color using food coloring or acrylic paint to get some pretty amazing effects. But oddly, no matter how cool a carved pumpkin is, I've found that folks are a notch less impressed with it if it's painted too much. When I'm set up at a table for a carving demo in public locations, folks will almost always walk right by a painted pumpkin to focus on a non-painted one, only noticing the painted one later. Maybe because if there's too much paint it stops being a pumpkin and starts just being "sculpture?" For that reason I usually try to stay subtle when I think something needs a little color, just a light wash to emphasize the shadows or make something a bit grosser. So I think it's more impactful to preserve plenty of pumpkin-ness. Leave some orange here and there, especially near the stem, and keep painted elements to a minimum.

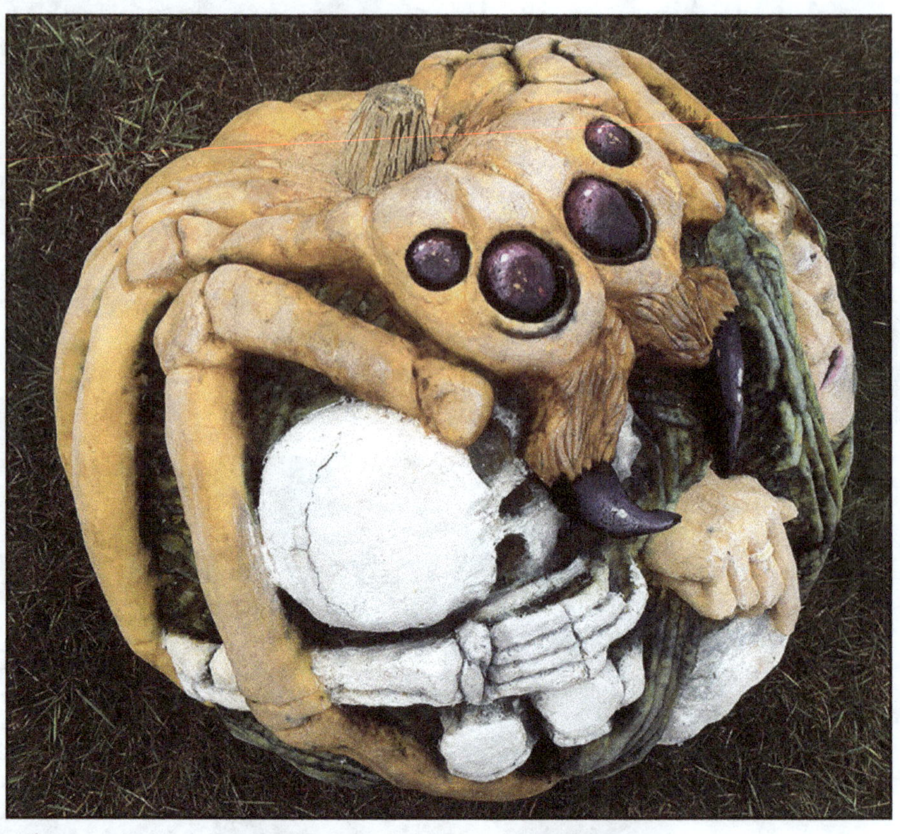

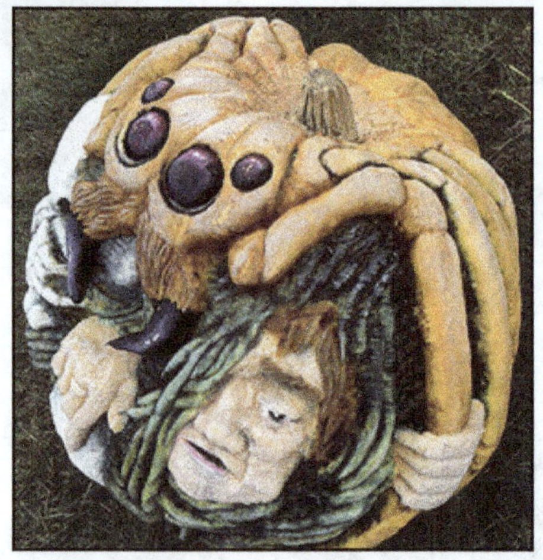

this spider crawled out of the dirt at shakefork family farms, 2017

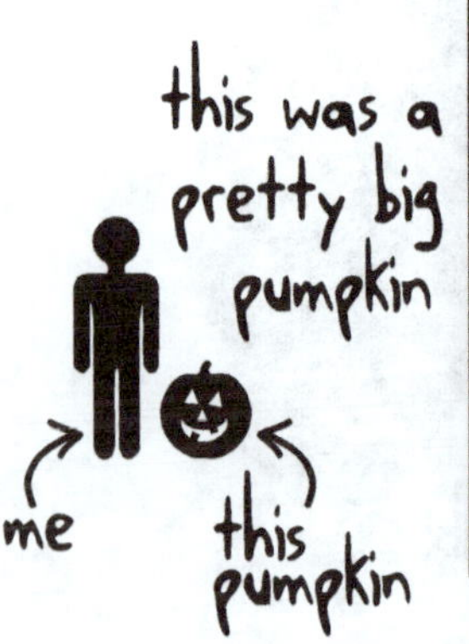

this was a pretty big pumpkin

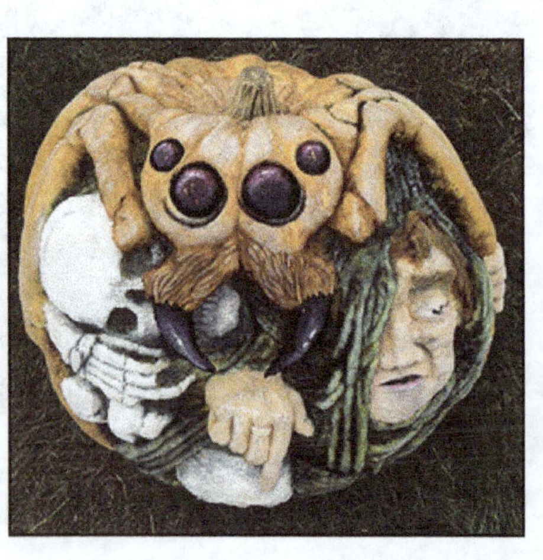

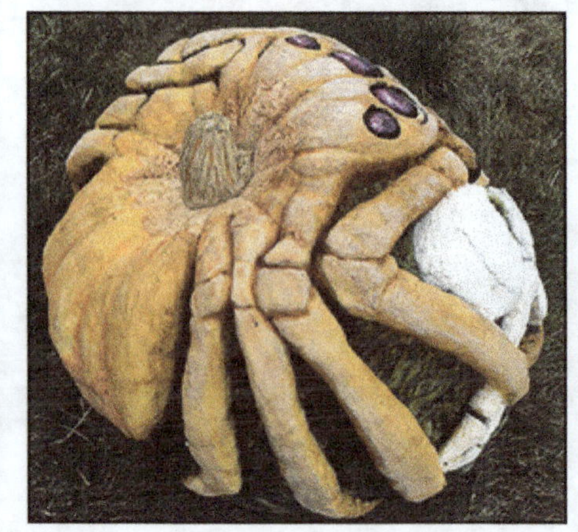

this lasted almost a month before it turned to mush. sometimes you get lucky!

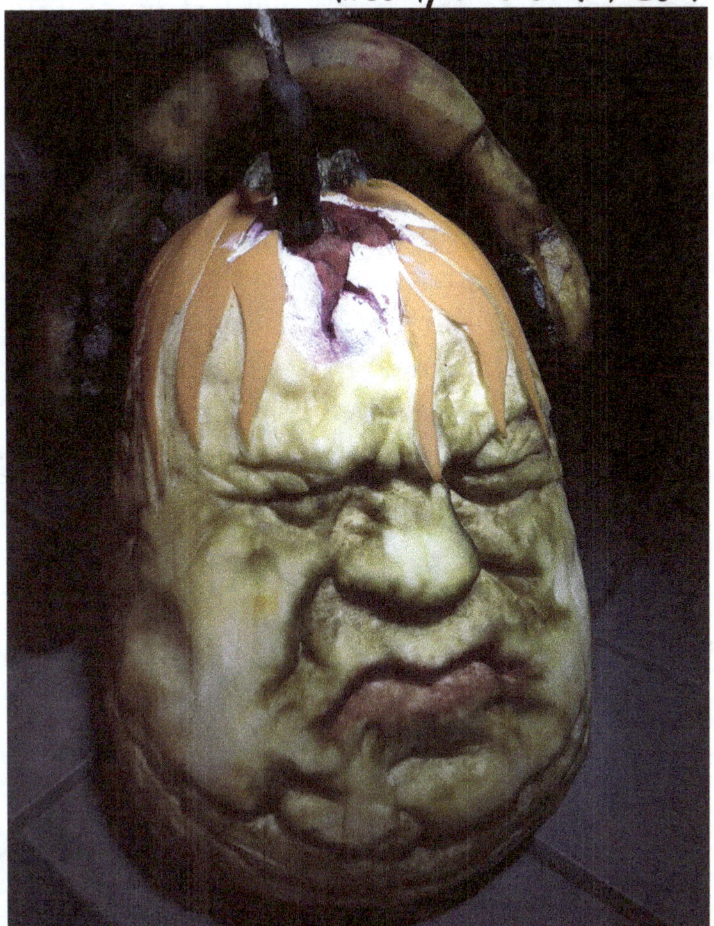

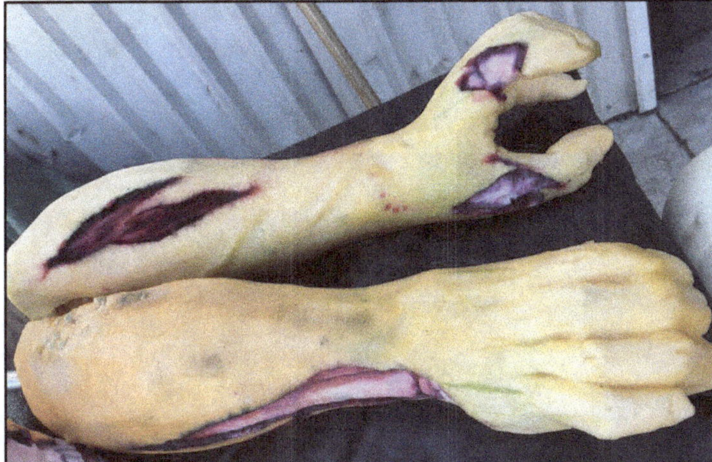

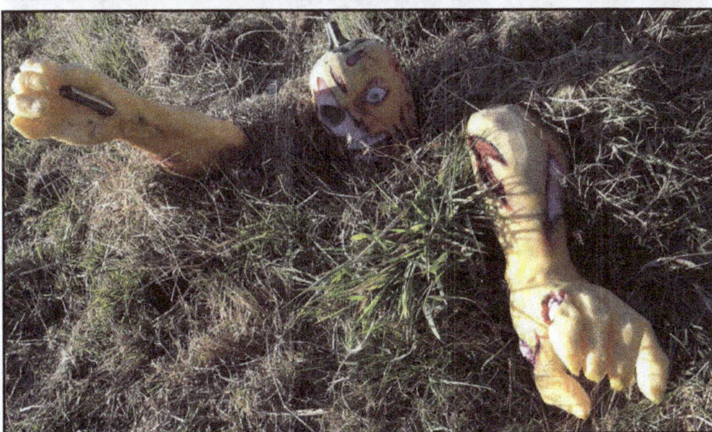

this zombie crawled out of the dirt at
organic matters ranch in 2017

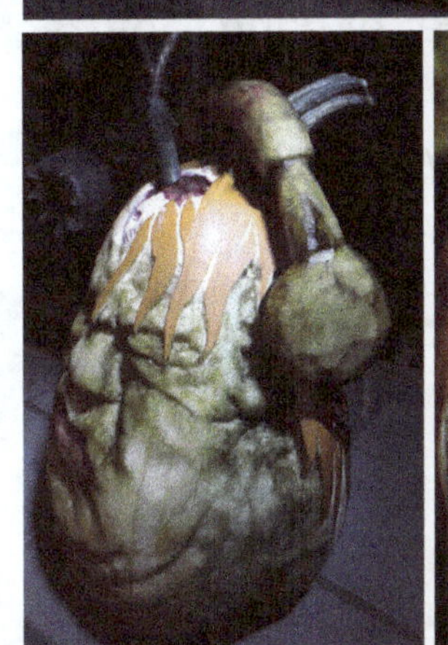

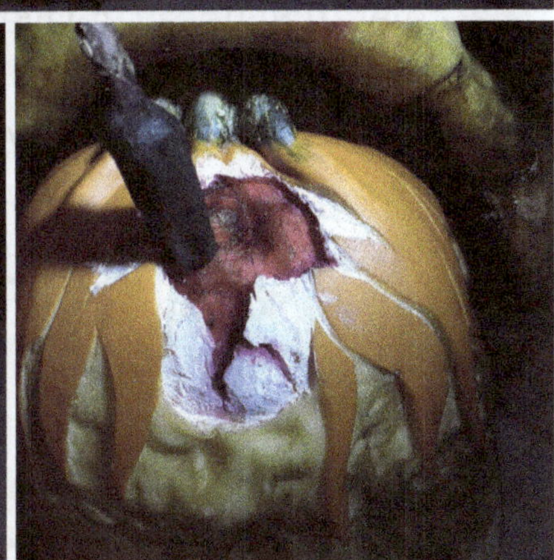

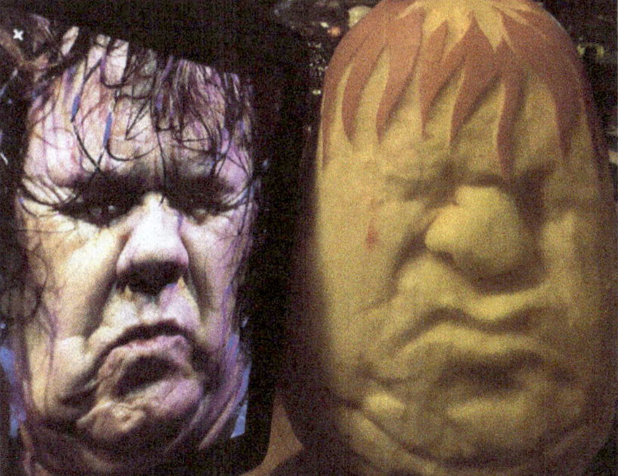

looking for
ideas?
do a web
image
search for
"guitar
face"

Pumpkin preservation

A 3D-sculpted pumpkin carved without breaking through to the inside will last up to four weeks if you're careful, and closer to one week if you're not. Sometimes if you can keep them out of direct sunlight in cool weather, they'll stick around for up to two weeks. But with care, you can keep your pumpkin "alive" for a month. Here's how:

1. Buying time: cover the carved surfaces of your pumpkin with plastic wrap and keep it refrigerated until you're ready to display it. A week or two later, it will still look as good as new! Extend the season further by letting it spend each night (or day) in the fridge, putting it on display only during peak viewing hours.

2. Preventing mold: You can extend its life a great deal by periodically spraying all the carved surfaces with bleach-based cleaner, or with vinegar (if you're composting and don't want to kill your good bugs). That will keep mold and fungi and other cooties from accelerating decay. A layer of hand sanitizer will help, and I've heard folks claim that a coating of vegetable oil will provide another barrier.

3. Pickling: Villafane Studios has pioneered pumpkin pickling, and Ray and his weirdo associates are often spotted submerging their carved masterpieces in aquariums and big spooky jars filled with a vinegar solution. Visit them at **villafanestudios.com**.

Pumpkins for posterity

What follows are a bunch of pumpkins I've carved over the years, in no particular order.

Visit **mikecraghead.com** for more pumpkins and other silly things.

Happy carving!

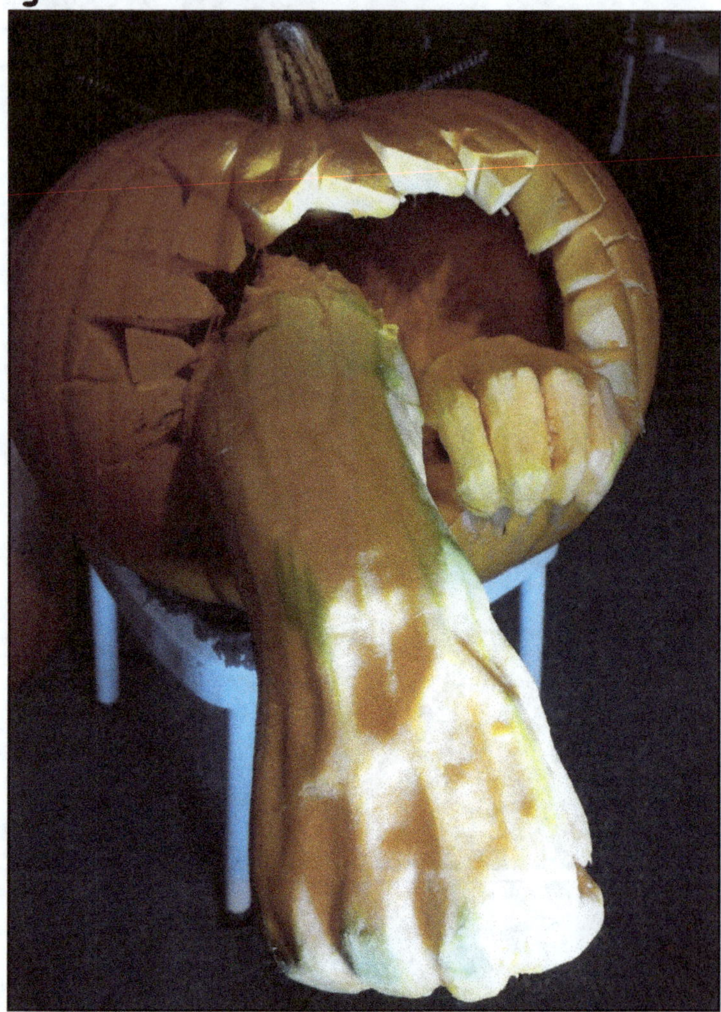

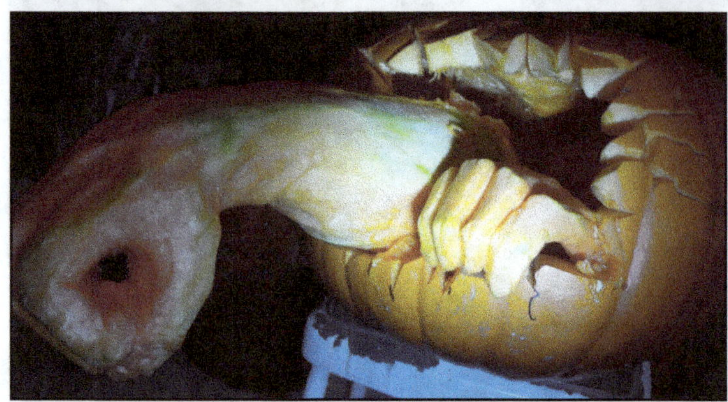

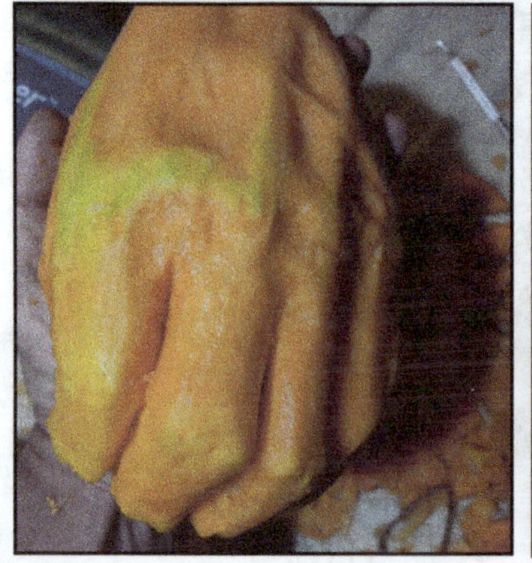

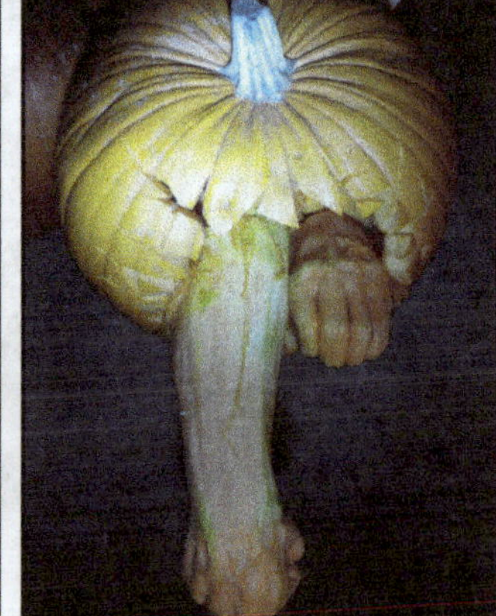

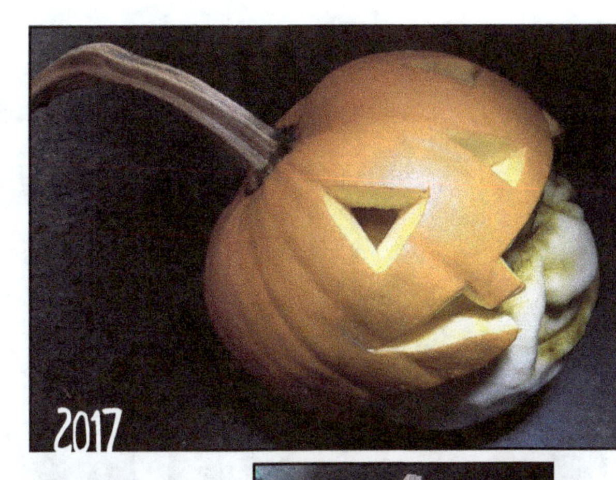
2017

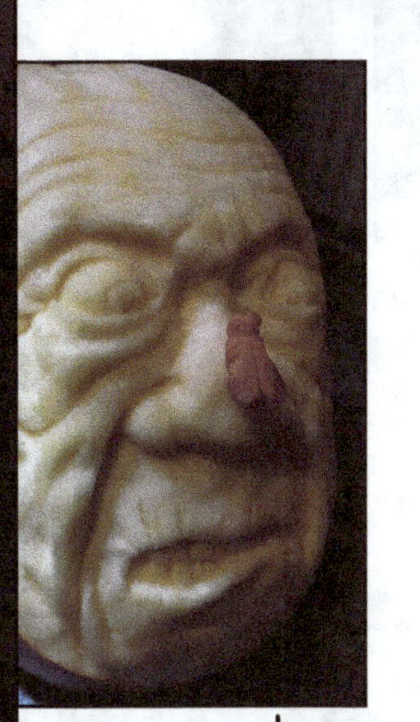
damn flies,
2017

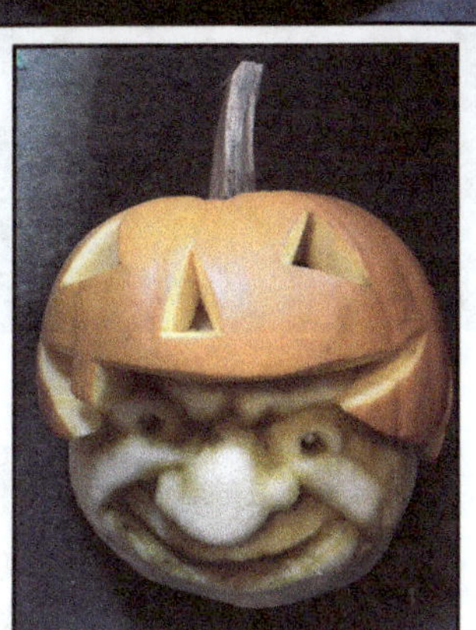

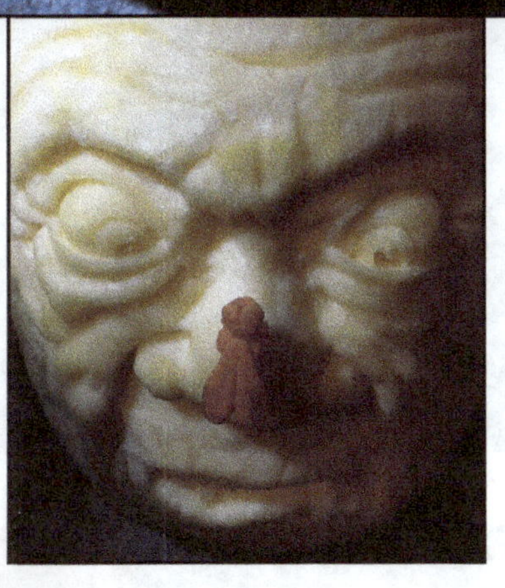

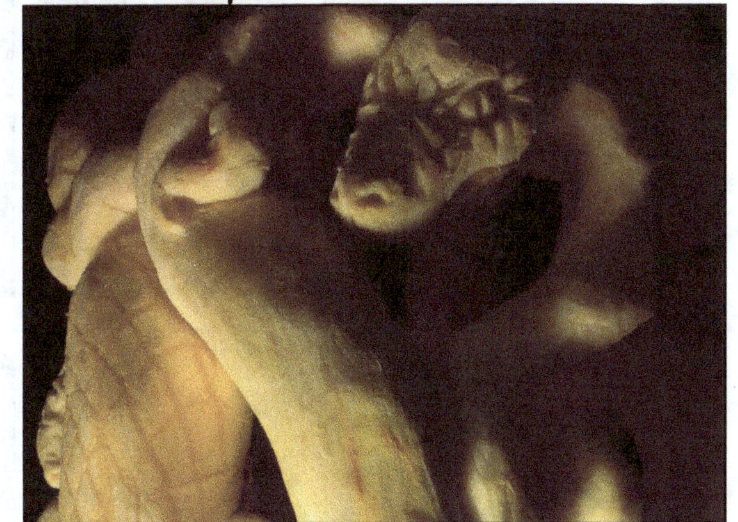
why'd it have to be snakes?! 2015

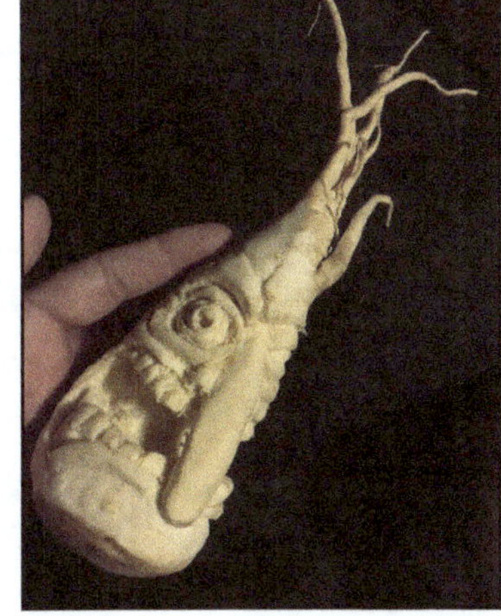
parsnip

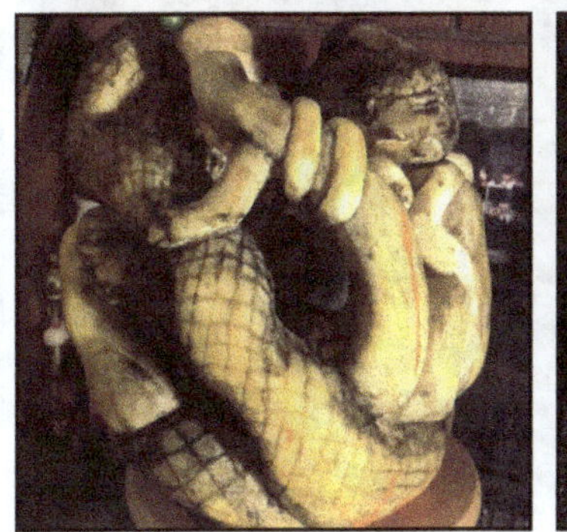

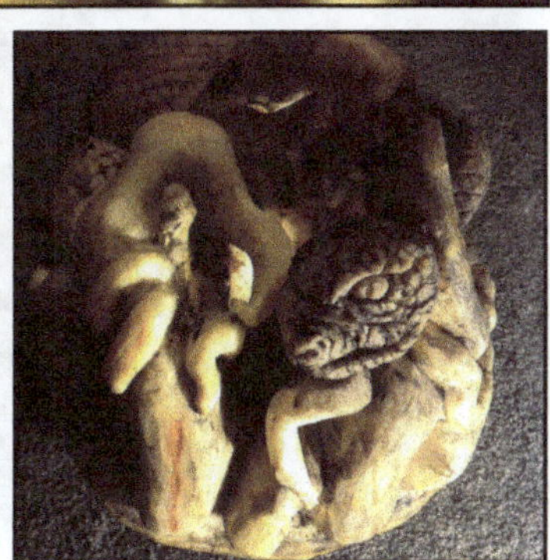

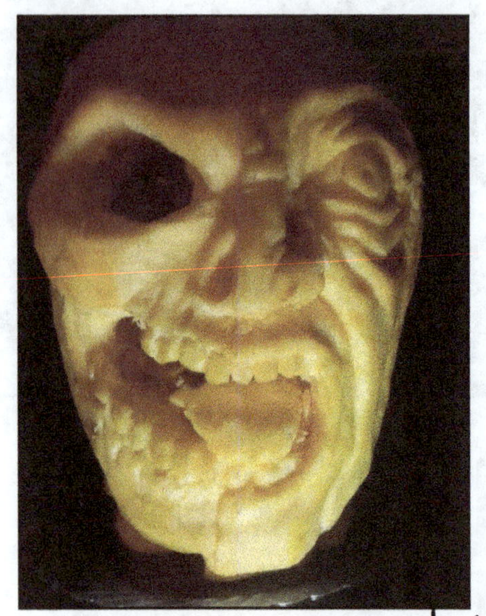 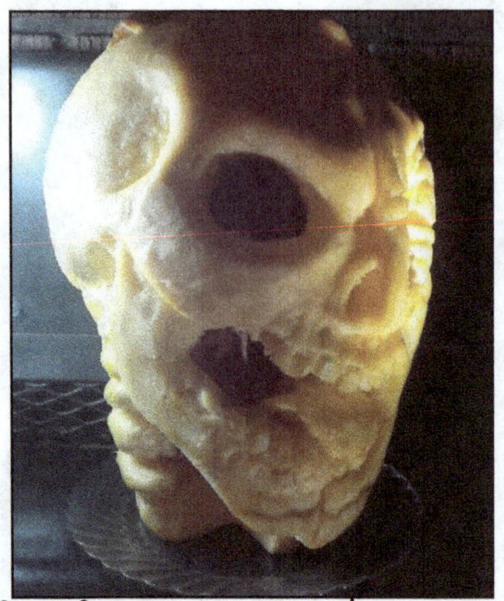 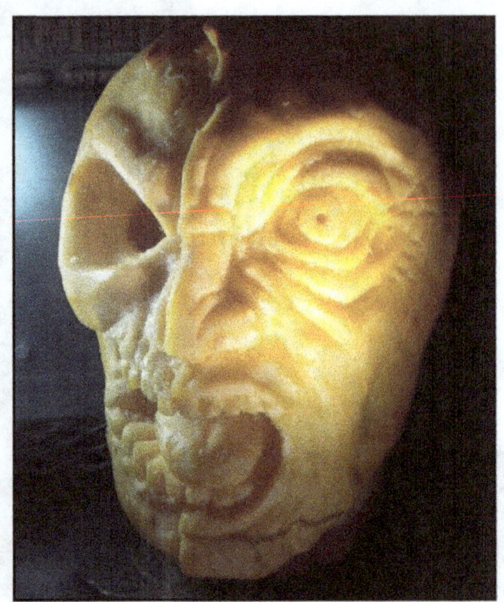

half a face is better than none, 2014

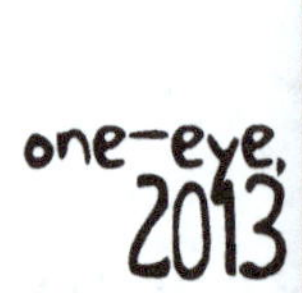 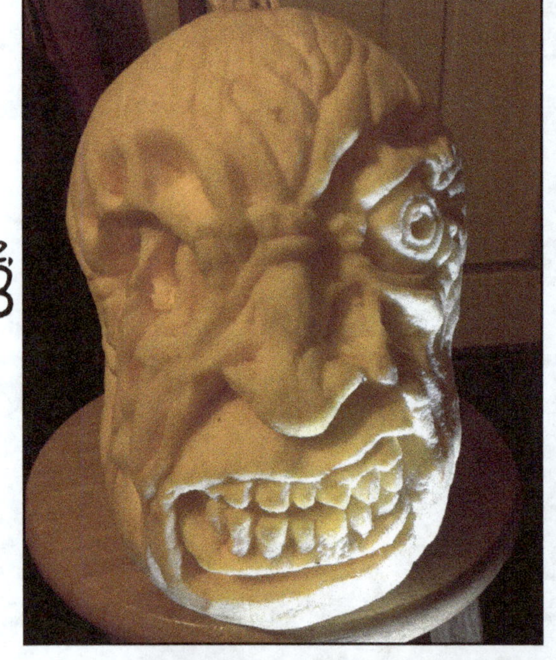

one-eye, 2013

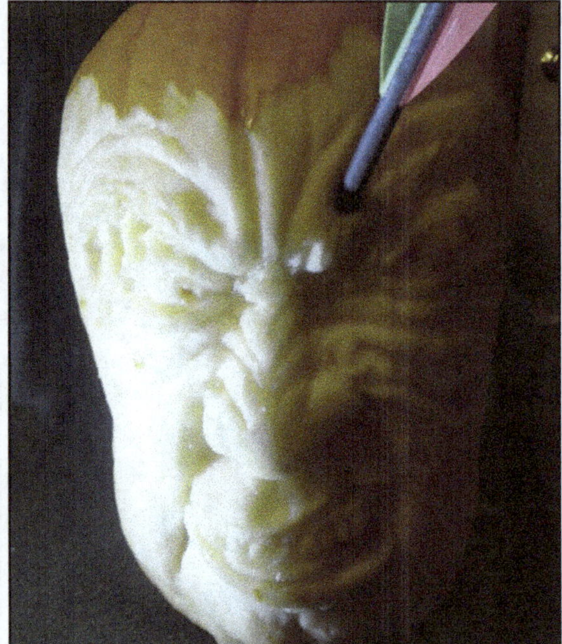

arrow-through-the-head, 2012

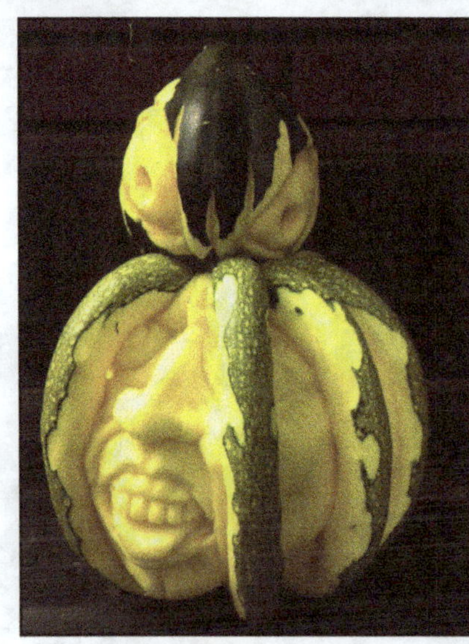

there's a squid on my head! 2011

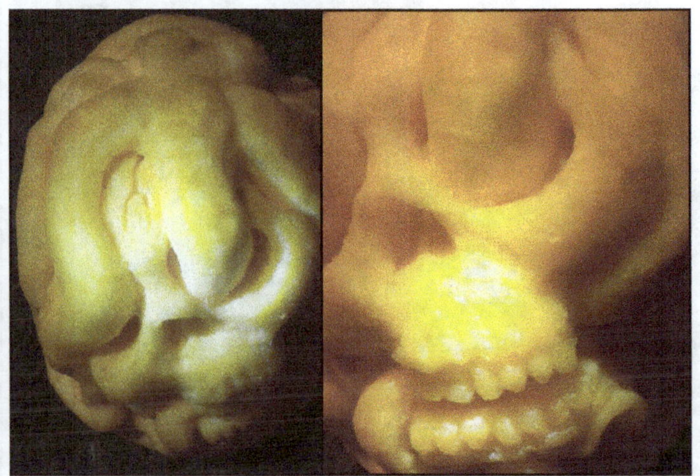

octopus vs. skull, 2015

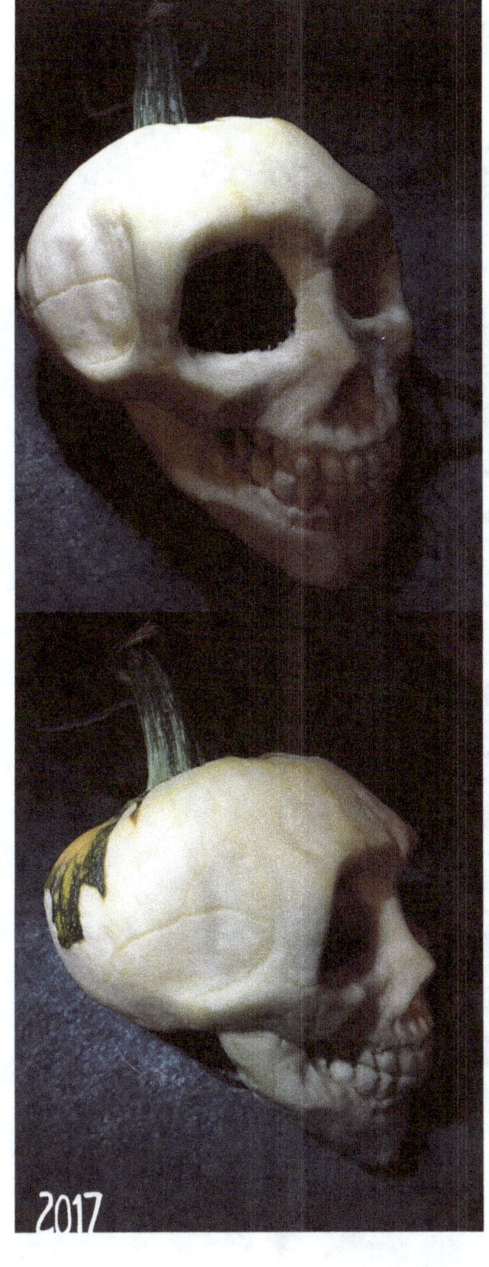

oh jeez, more skulls?!

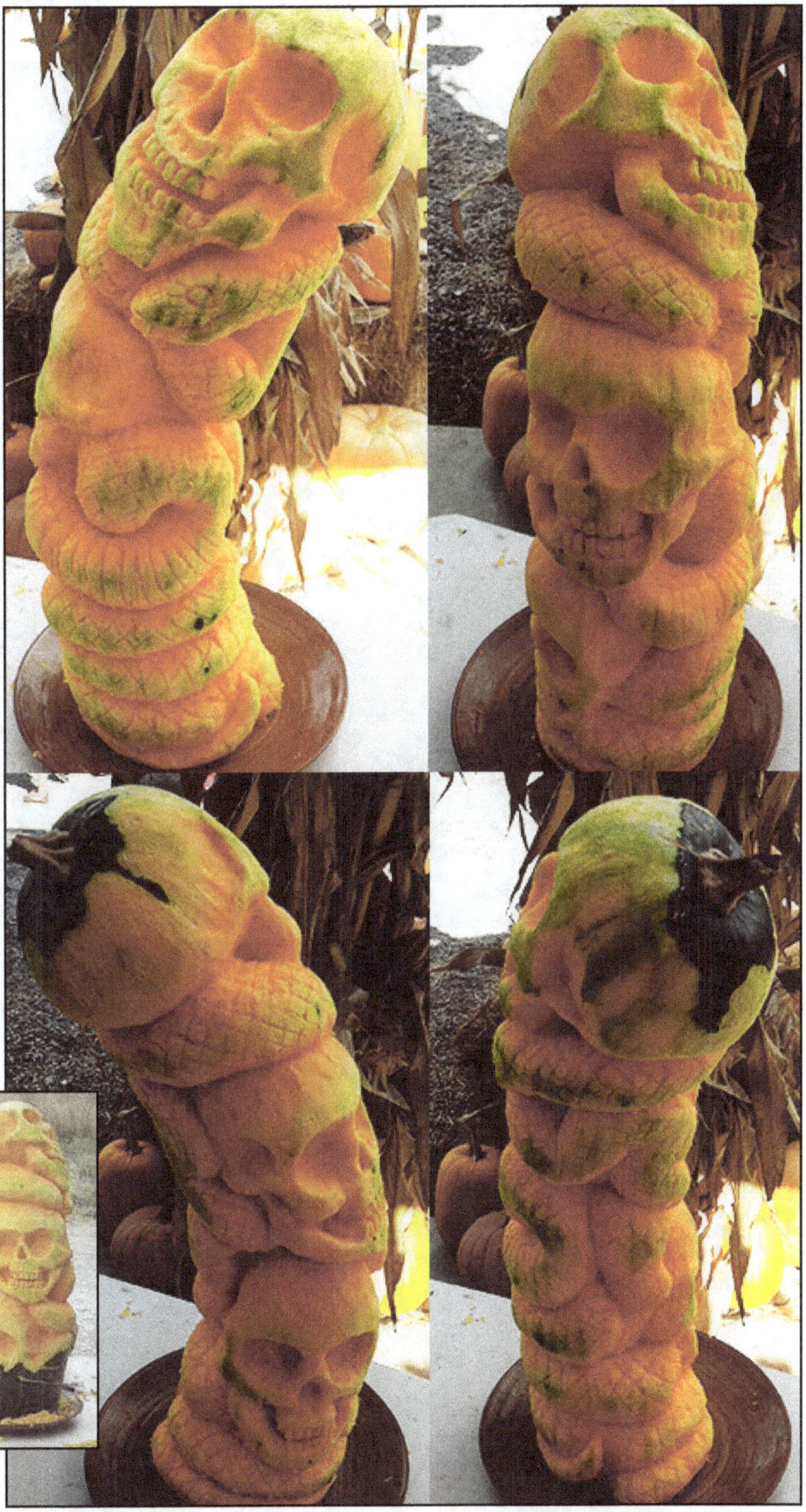

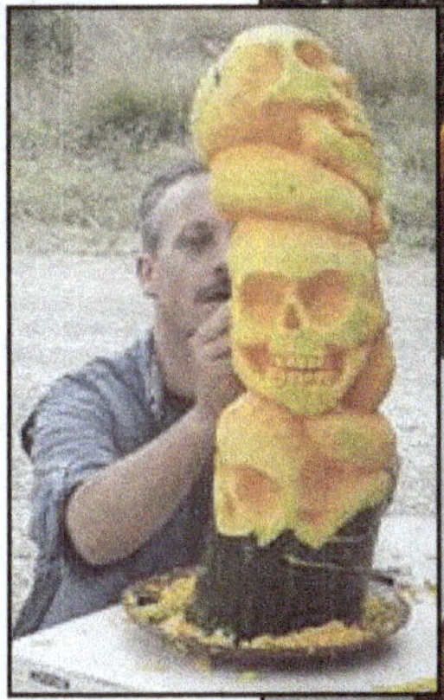

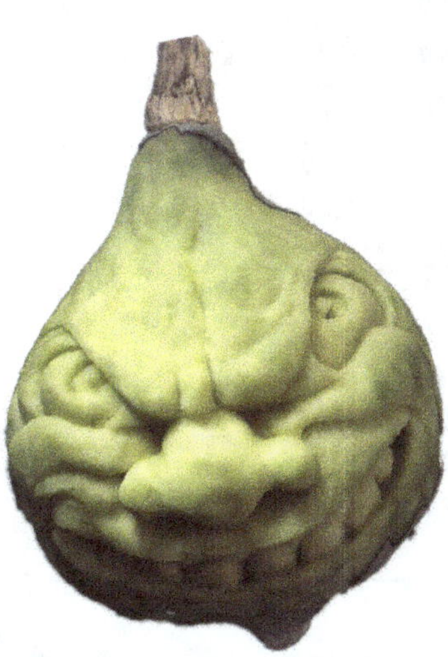

mean hubbard, 2017

snakes and skulls, 2015

carnivorous pumpkin, 2012.
this pumpkin was pretty big. not as big as
the one on page 36, but still pretty big

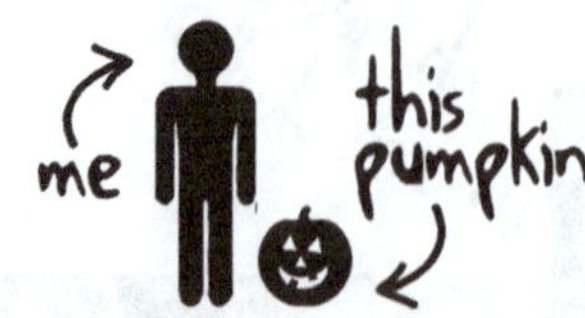

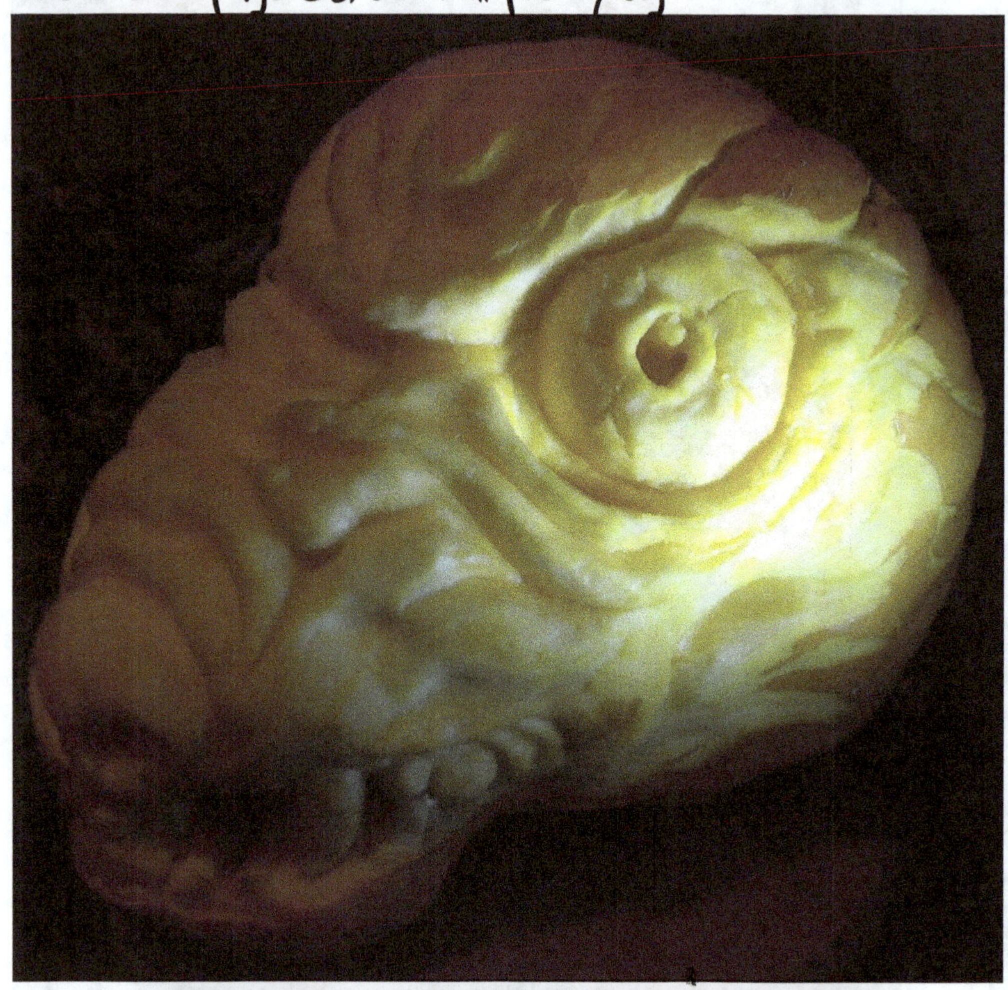

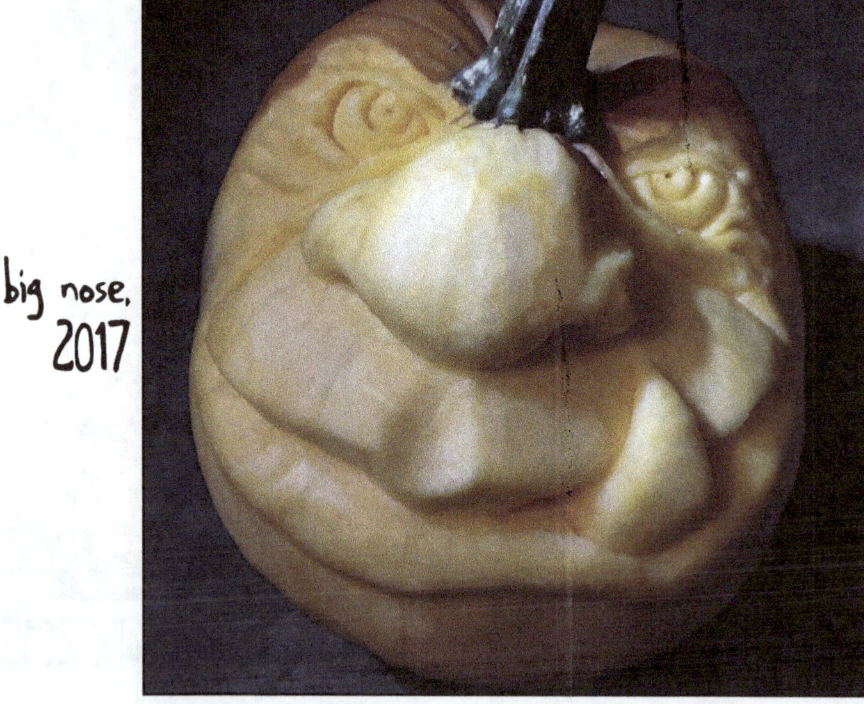

big nose,
2017

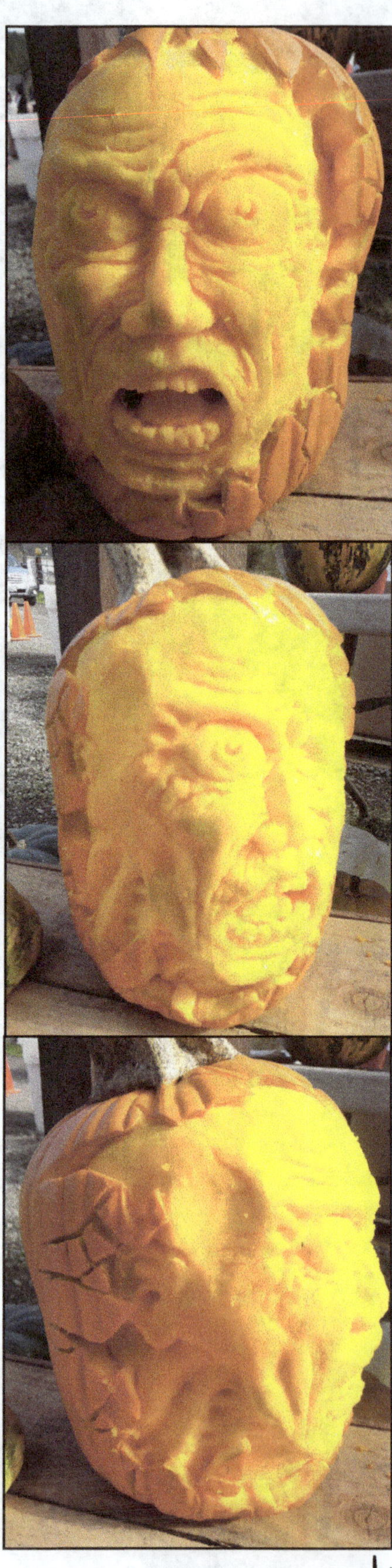

agh!
2016

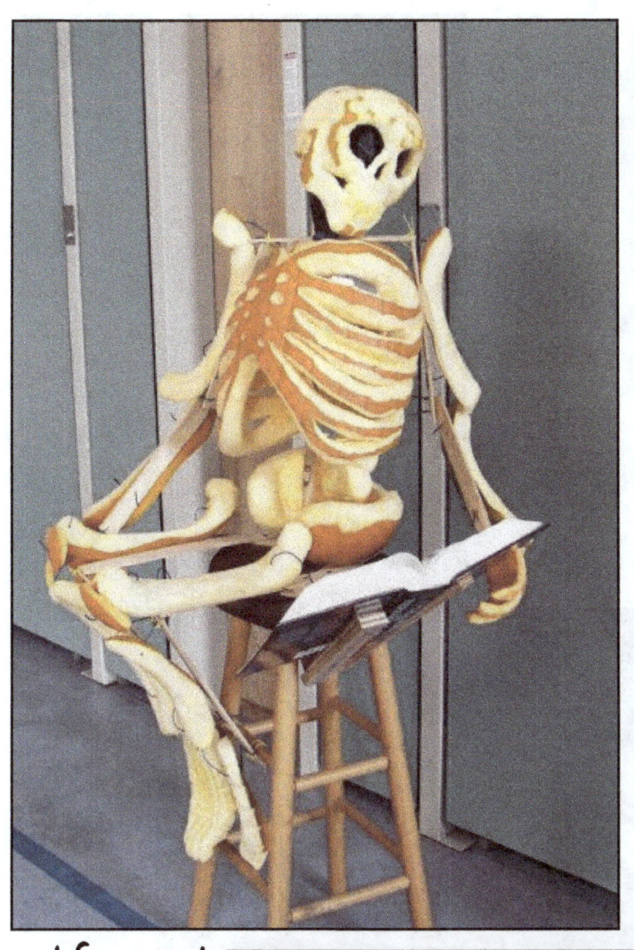

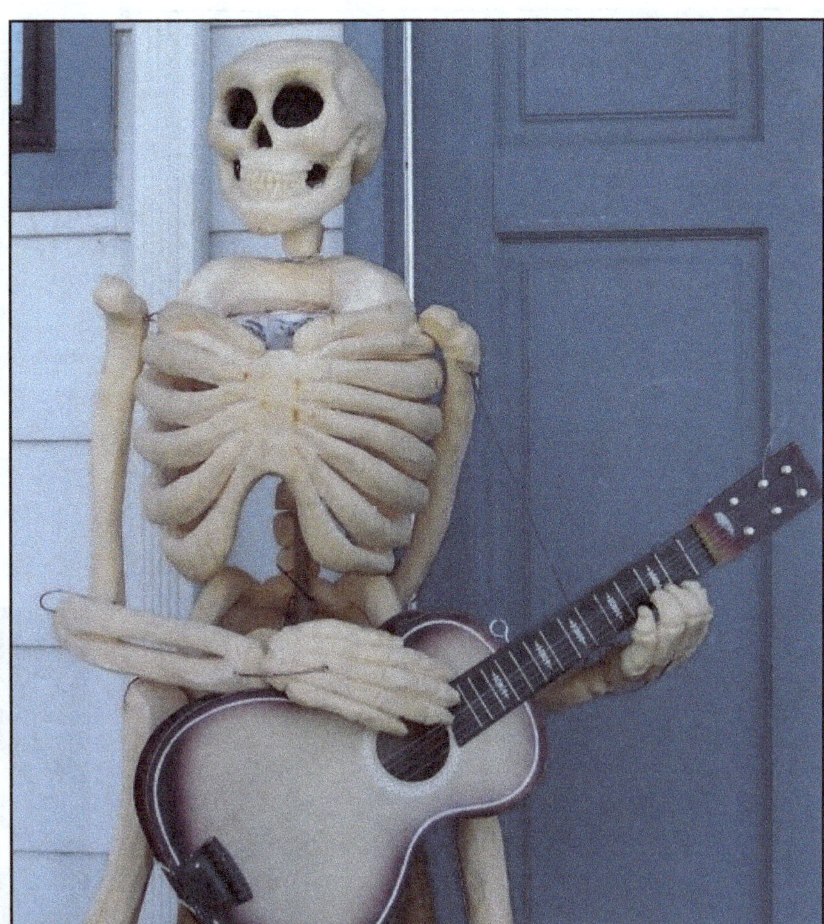

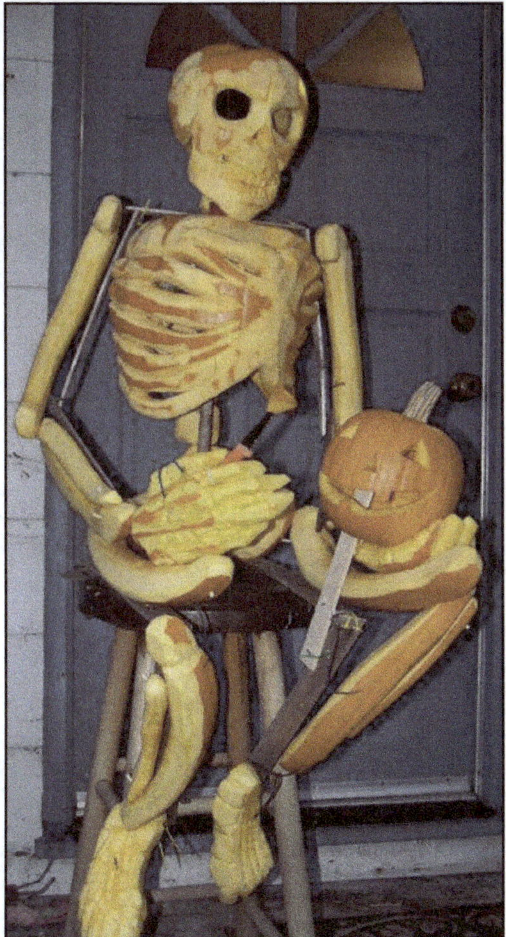

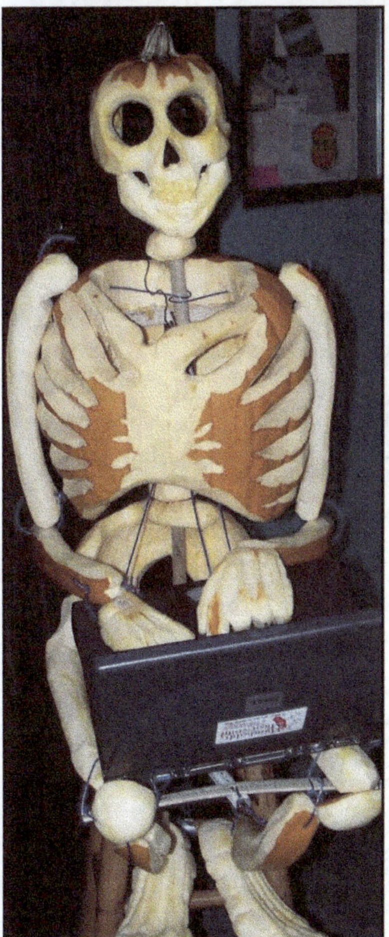

because the skull is the first part to mushify, i usually make at least two skulls so i can swap one out and extend the "life" of a skeleton.

stuart,
2017

jerry,
2017

2017

stuart
has cool
hair

jerry
has no
hair

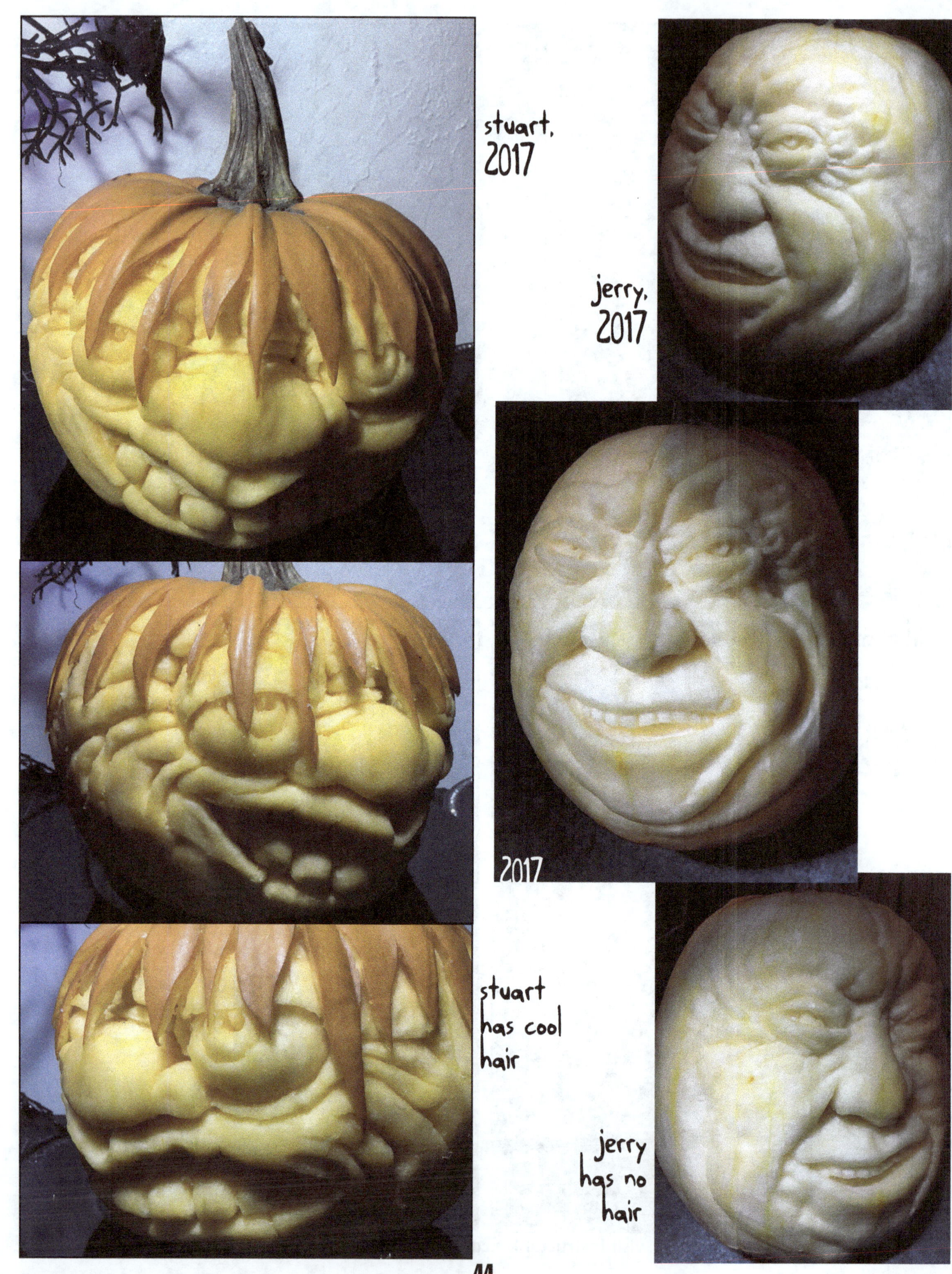

44

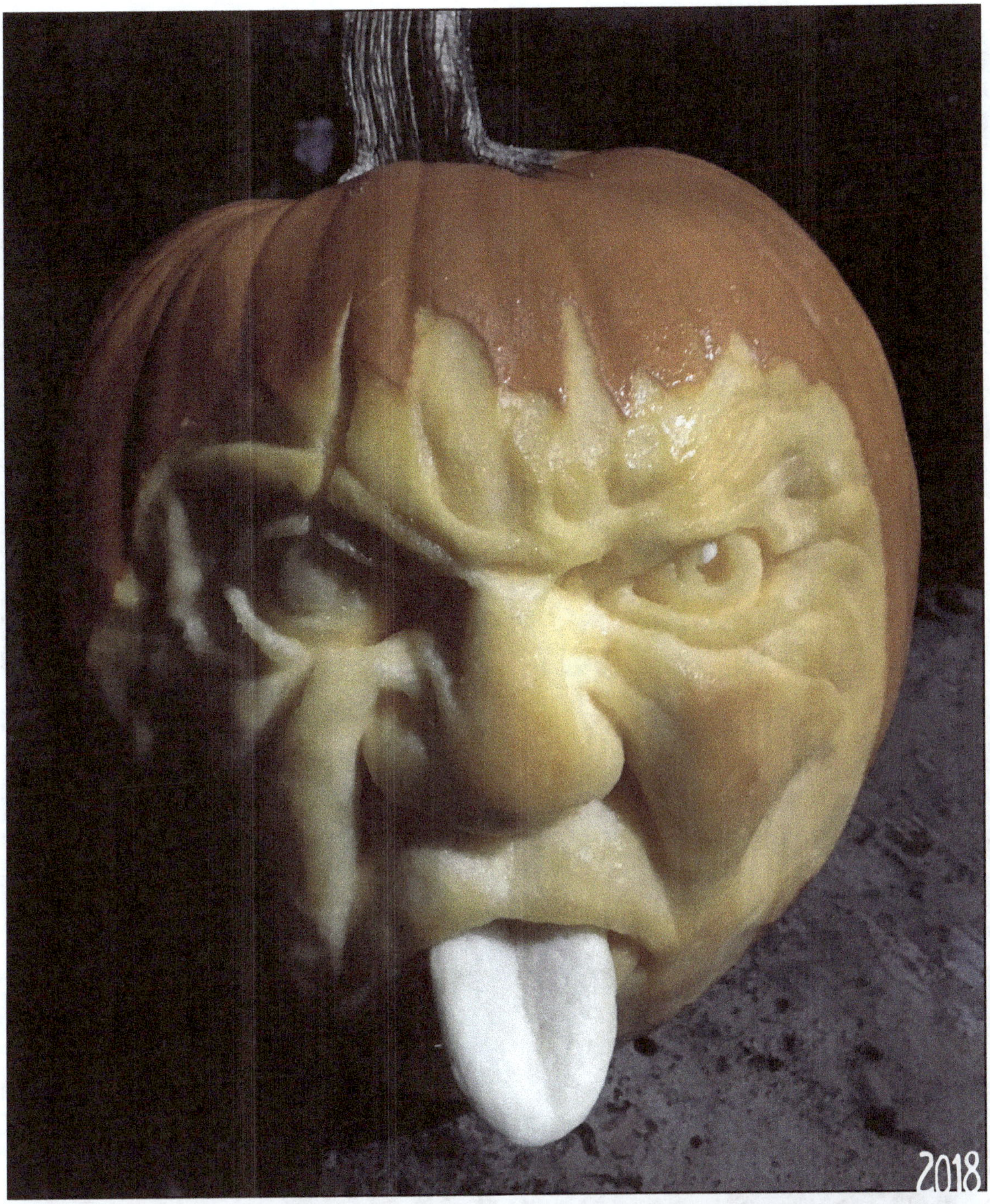

keep a turnip handy
for adding white
stuff like bugs or
eyeball sparkles or
whatever.

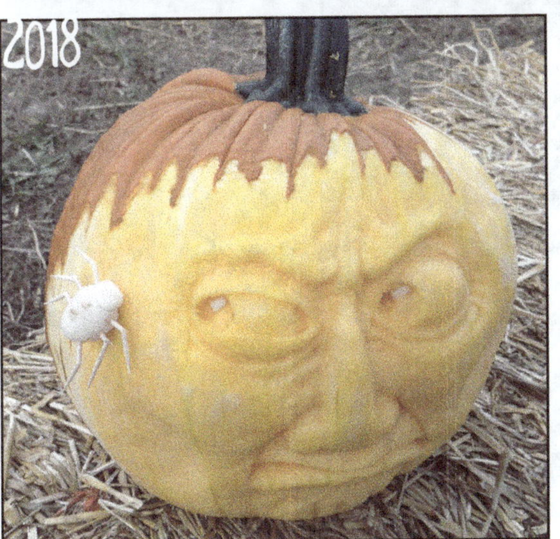

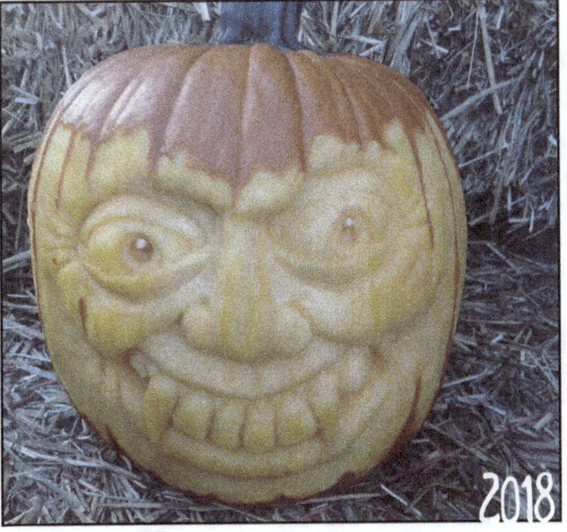

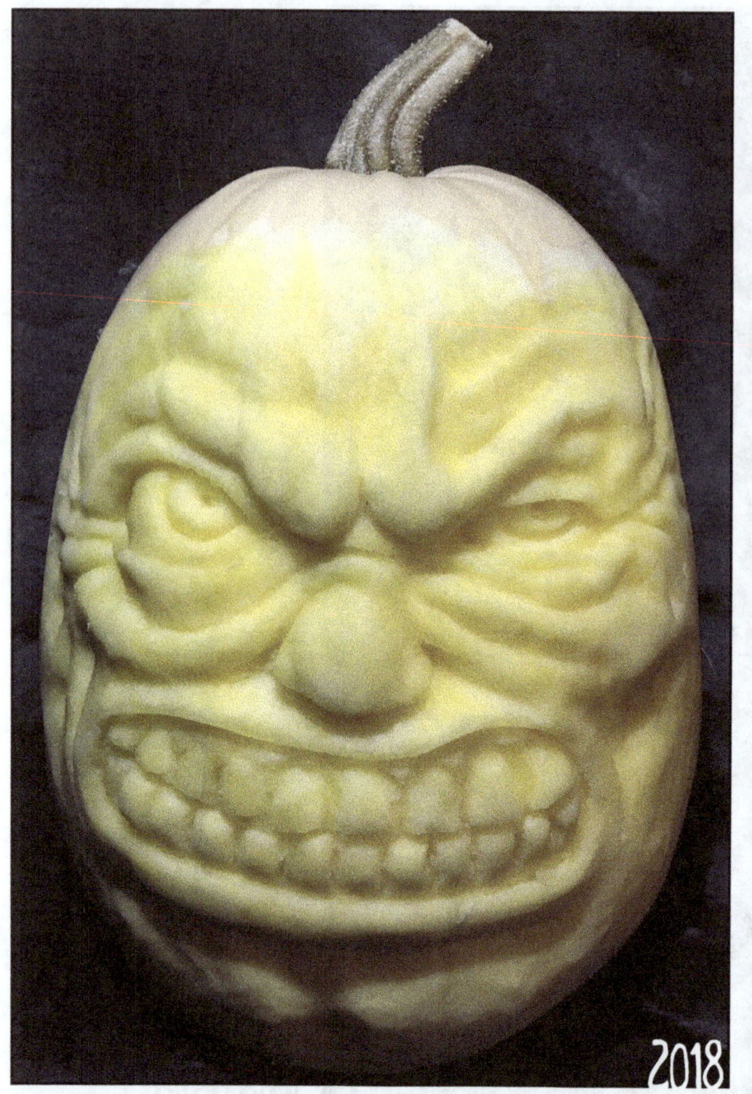

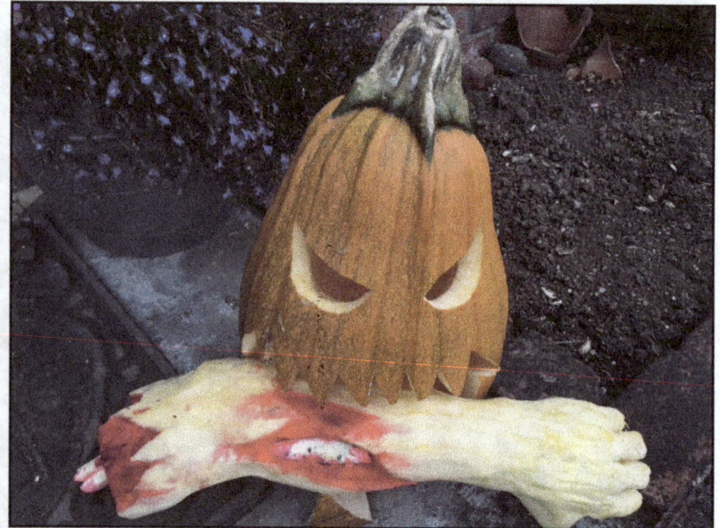

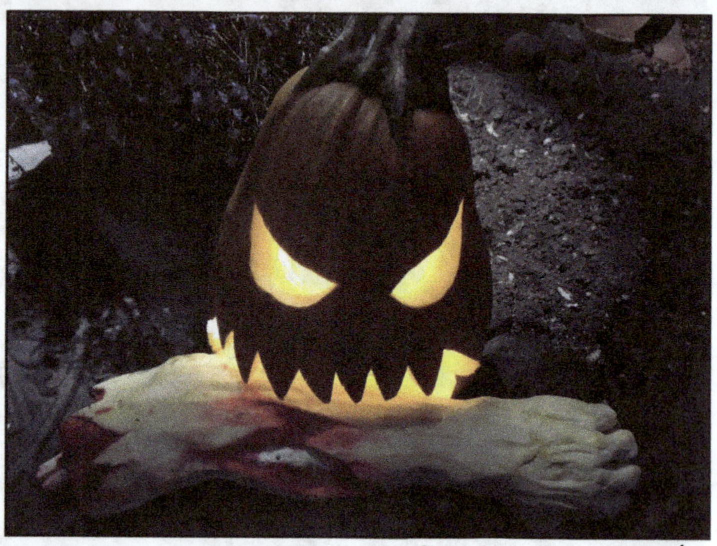

2018

in 2018 i fed another arm to another pumpkin, like i did on page 33.

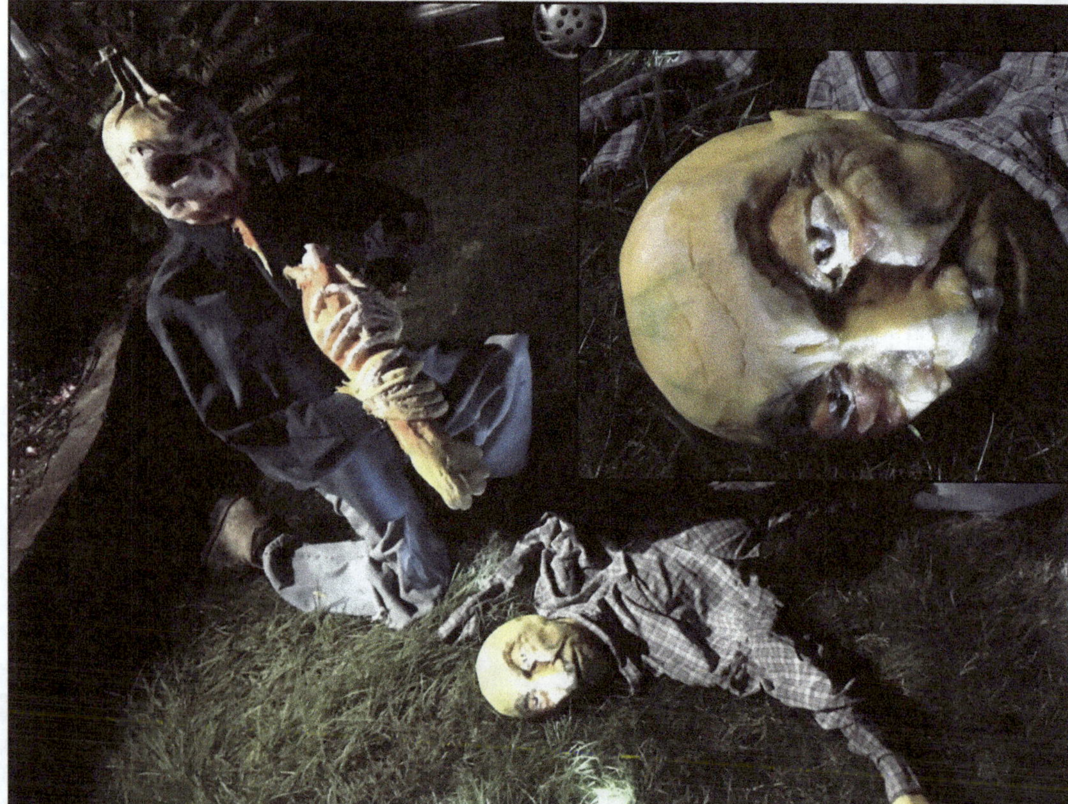

this pumpkin-headed zombie ate a guy on my lawn in 2018.

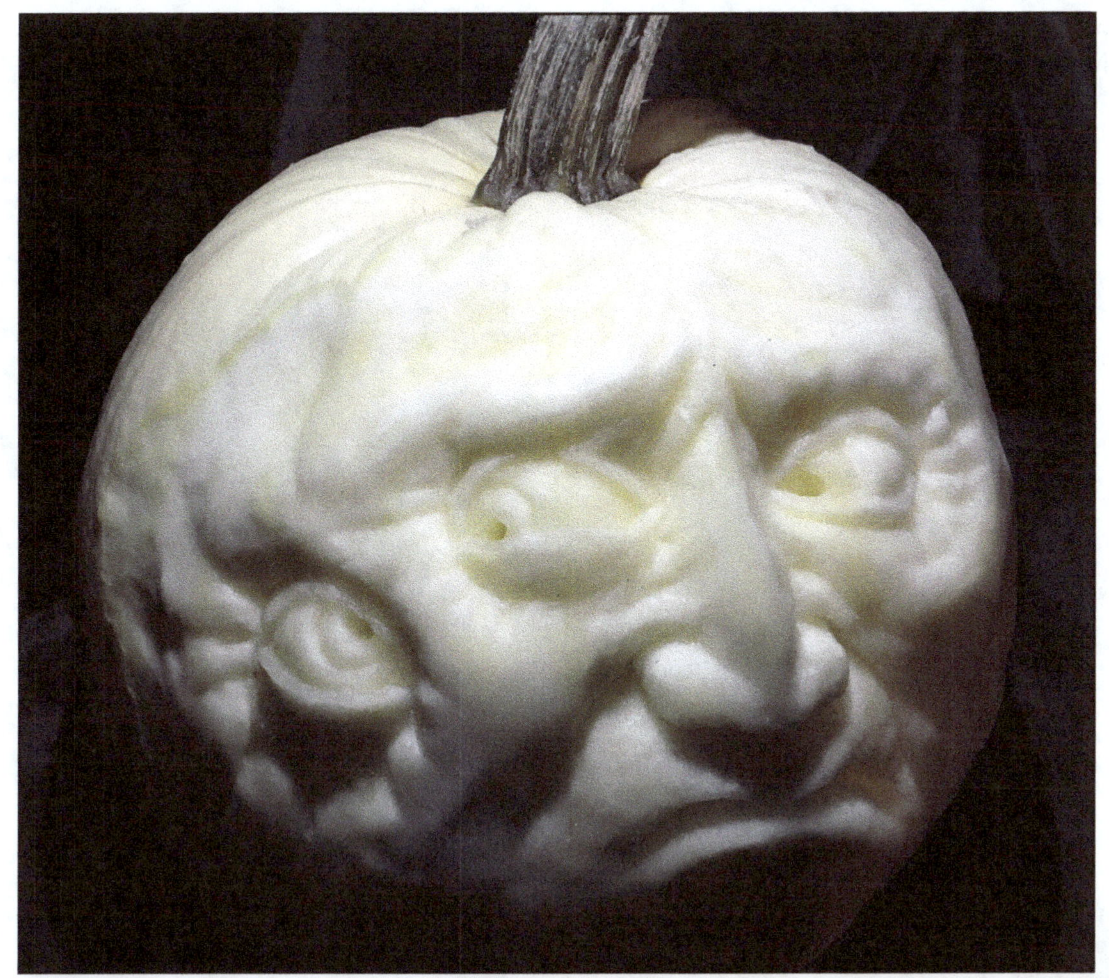

extra eye,
not sure why
2018

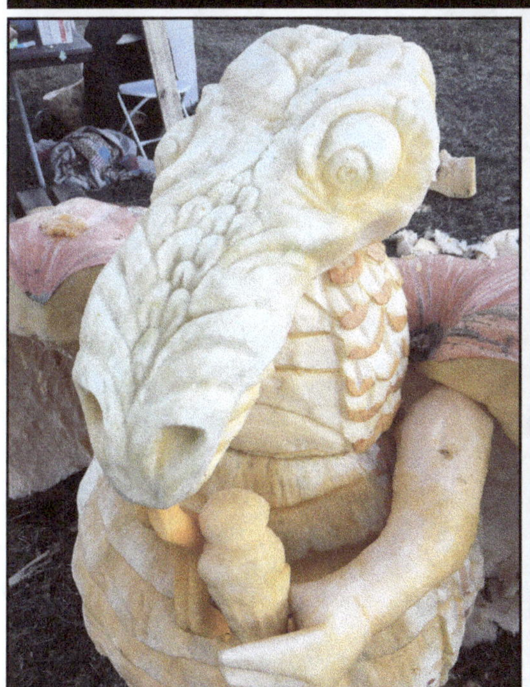

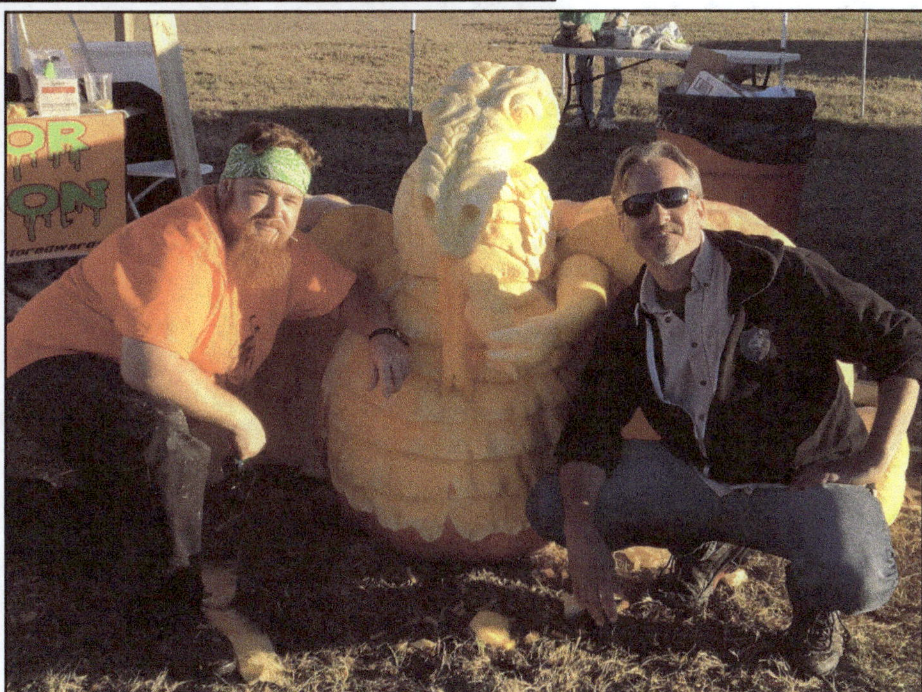

the weber family pumpkin festival in ohio is a very cool event run by cool people and you should definitely go there. in 2018, tator edwards and i got to carve a dragon eating an ice cream cone, using an 1100 pound pumpkin. in the picture on the right, tator is the one with the green bandanna, i'm the one with the sunglasses, and the dragon is the one with the ice cream cone.

Below is a collage of photos of my snow sculptures. They were all
taken during a blizzard so they're pretty hard to see, sorry about that.

Hi, I'm Mike. I live in Eureka, California, which is so far north it might as well be Oregon. I play music, and I like to carve things and make stuff.

In 2017, I was lucky to be on a Halloween-themed cable TV show where I was the pumpkin part of a sugar-cake-pumpkin team. I am equally proud and embarrassed by that experience, having created some pretty cool things under pressure, and also having made some utterly moronic mistakes. But Im grateful for the friends and memories I made there, and I assure you that the literal and emotional scars have fully healed.

Just don't watch season 7 of that show. Or do. No, wait - don't.

My biggest takeaway from that experience was that I had a lot more to learn. A new set of challenges is built in to every pumpkin: to crank up the quality, variety, and speed of your carving. So, I studied up on sculpture and portraiture, and when pumpkin season rolled around again, I carved more than I ever had.

And I got better. I'd do public pumpkin carving demos where I could meet folks and they could point and laugh and throw rotten fruit at me. I'd answer questions and encourage folks who were interested in trying to up their pumpkin game, and they'd take pictures of my carvings or thumb through a few pages of pumpkin photos I'd brought. But I wanted to be able to offer them something more tangible, that they could bring home and use and/or inflict upon their more pumpkin-centric friends and family. So that's where this book came from. I hope it helps, I hope you like it, and I hope next time you throw fruit at me you'll lay off the rotten apples a bit, because those can really explode on impact.

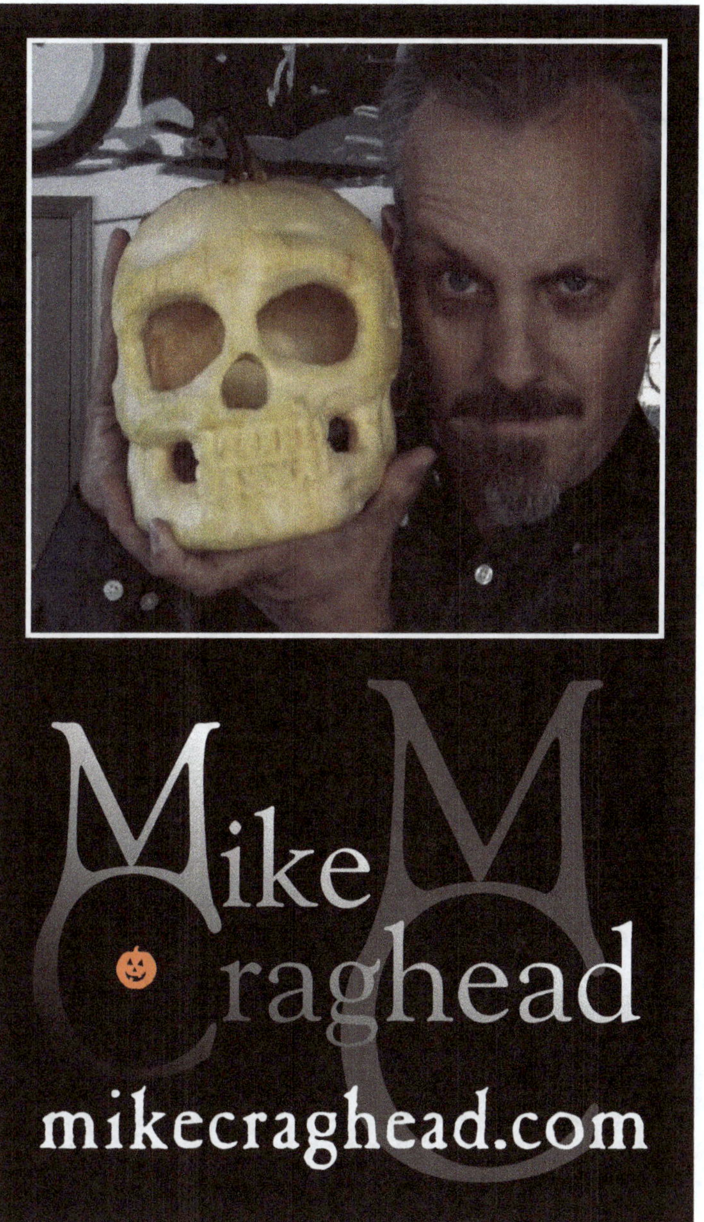

mikecraghead.com

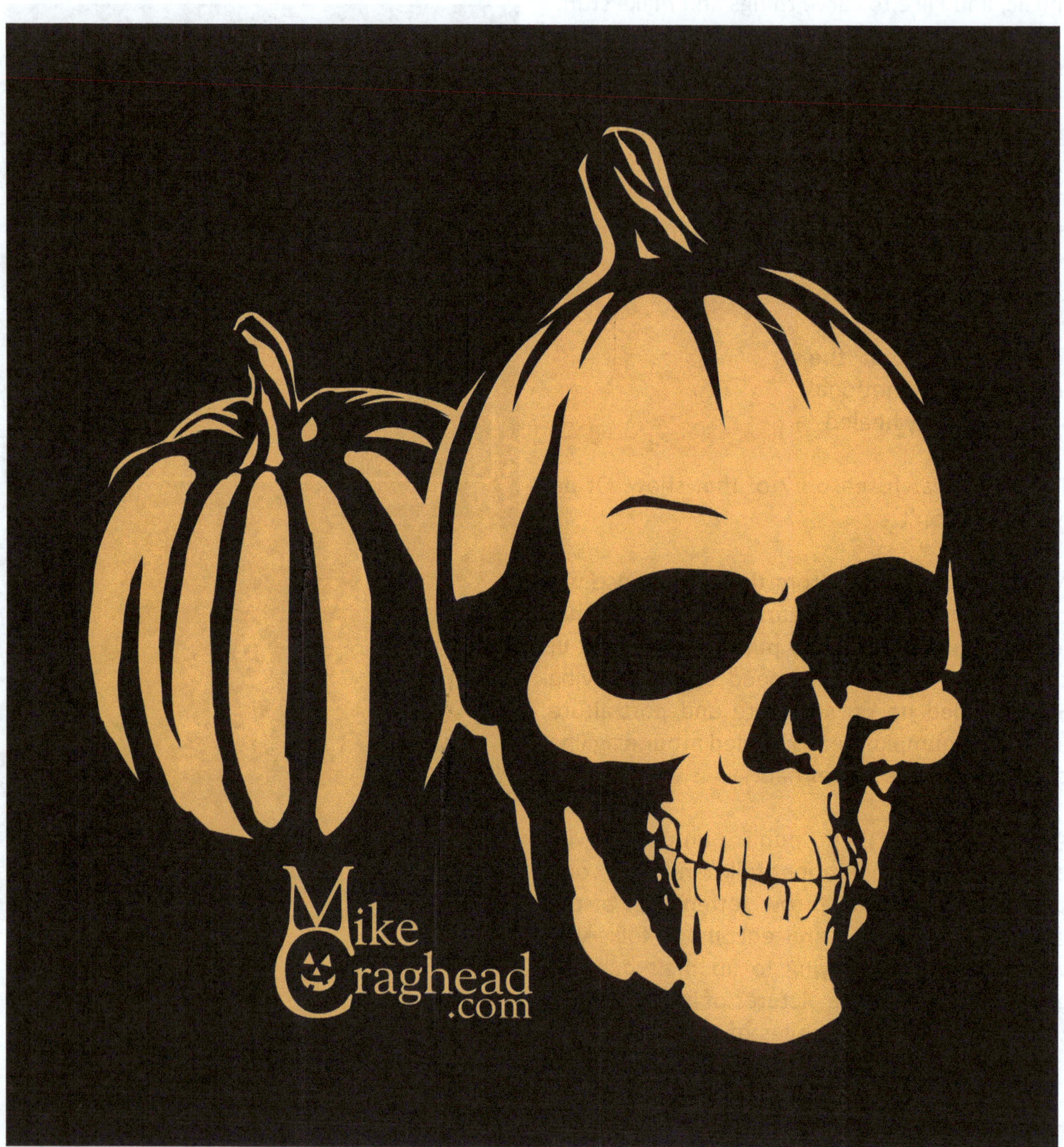
Mike
Craghead
.com

www.ingramcontent.com/pod-product-compliance
Lightning Source LLC
Chambersburg PA
CBHW080311030726
47593CB00009B/2715